T0309220

Conflict Management and Leadership Development Using Mediation

A Volume in
Contemporary Issues in Conflict Management and Dialogue

Series Editors:
Nance T Algert, *Texas A&M University*
Carla Liau-Hing Yep, *The Center for Change and Conflict Resolution*
Kenita S. Rogers, *Texas A&M University*
Christine A. Stanley, *Texas A&M University*

Contemporary Issues
in Conflict Management and Dialogue

Nance T Algert, Carla Liau-Hing Yep,
Kenita S. Rogers, and Christine A. Stanley, Series Editors

Critical Dialogues in Higher Education (2020)
by Nance T Algert and Clare A. Gill

Conflict Management and Leadership Development Using Mediation

By

Nance T Algert
Texas A&M University

Information Age Publishing, Inc.
Charlotte, North Carolina • www.infoagepub.com

Library of Congress Cataloging-in-Publication Data

CIP data for this book can be found on the Library of Congress website:
http://www.loc.gov/index.html

Paperback: 978-1-64802-259-3
Hardcover: 978-1-64802-260-9
E-Book: 978-1-64802-261-6

Printed in the United States of America.

CONTENTS

PREFACE

Nance T Algert
The Center for Change and Conflict Resolution

This book uses the conflict intervention called mediation, which helps one become a stronger conflict manager. It presents general knowledge for basic mediation and is particularly effective for training new mediators. This book is best utilized in conjunction with a formal mediation training course that is taught by a mediator instructor and is designed to supplement the 40-hour training standards as recommended by the Alternative Dispute Resolution section of the State Bar of Texas. The contents of this book reflect areas of importance addressed in conflict management and mediation training: review of conflict literature, alternative dispute resolution practices, the mediation format, and skill sets needed by the mediator.

It is always valuable to productively engage in conflict. The outcomes of engagement can have significant positive consequences, both for the individual and for the organization.

Through self-awareness, people can more effectively manage their conflicts and, therefore, their professional and personal relationships. By discussing issues related to conflict management, organizations can establish an expected protocol to be followed by individuals when in conflict. Most people are interested in and willing to resolve their conflicts. They simply need the appropriate skill set and the parameters for practicing these skill sets.

Self-awareness is essential for an individual to be an effective mediator, so readers are challenged to reflect upon their own biases and beliefs that

Conflict Management and Leadership Development Using Mediation
pp. ix–x
Copyright © 2021 by Information Age Publishing
All rights of reproduction in any form reserved.

may positively or negatively impact the mediation process. Awareness also involves understanding issues related to diversity, social justice, differences among individuals, and personal strengths and weaknesses in communication. Most important, self-awareness requires that the individual understands their own mental, emotional, physical, spiritual, and psychological state at a given moment so that they can be fully present to the disputants.

Besides a knowledge base of the process, a good mediator must be neutral, ready, adaptive, and skilled if they are going to facilitate resolution, rather than escalation of conflict.

For additional support in using this book, contact The Center for Change and Conflict Resolution at http://www.cccrtx.us/

INTRODUCTION

Mediate and mediation are derived from the Latin word *medius*, which means "the middle." The *Merriam-Webster Dictionary* gives us:

> **Mediate** \me-de-at vb –at ed; -at ing; 1: to interpose between parties in order to reconcile them 2: to reconcile differences.

By definition, the action of a mediator is to place oneself in the middle of a conflict. There are many processes available to aid individuals in reconciling conflicts. In judicial situations in the United States, various alternatives to dispute resolution are defined. Examples include mediation, negotiation, and arbitration. This book focuses on mediation.

For the purposes of this book, mediation is defined as a voluntary process in which the disputants strive to find a satisfactory resolution to their dispute. The mediator serves as a facilitator for this process and helps the disputants reach an agreement. The mediator does not impose solutions, assess punishment, administer judgment, decide who is right, or persuade the parties to accept any side of the dispute.

The mediator skill set includes anger management, conflict resolution, neutrality, active listening, creativity, and mastery of a guided process to facilitate the mediation. Mediation between cooperative disputants requires that the parties agree to:

- express their feelings and points of view;
- identify their needs;
- clarify issues;
- understand the other party's view; and
- explore solutions.

Conflict Management and Leadership Development Using Mediation
pp. xi–xii

The goal for the disputants is to be able to negotiate an agreement that is satisfactory to both parties.

We have organized this book to:

1. present a brief perspective on change in the workplace and the stress and conflicts that often accompany change;
2. share a framework for understanding conflict and typical behavior patterns when individuals are dealing with conflict. With this framework in mind, the reader can begin to understand the processes and role that a mediator should use to operate in "the middle" of a conflict without getting pulled into the conflict;
3. highlight several tools for the mediator to use in a mediation process; and
4. identify aspects of a mediation training program for those striving to preempt the potential of costly conflicts by having known mediators available.

CHAPTER 1

CHANGE AND THE WORKPLACE

It has been said many times that the one constant in life is that change will occur. For each individual, changes occur both internally and externally. Internally, our feelings, emotions, commitments, and attitudes are examples of aspects that vary under different conditions. Externally, the people around us are changing constantly, as are organizations, environments, and the tools available to navigate the change.

Sometimes, we are responsible for the change and at other times the change is imposed upon us. We may desire to change jobs and may activate an effort to search, interview, and move into a new job; on the contrary, a change imposed on us would be a "layoff" that forces us to leave our current job.

When change occurs, whether perceived as positive or negative and whether self-imposed or driven by someone else, there are a few common variables that always accompany change. Specifically, change is always accompanied by varying levels of resistance, stress, conflict, and altered behaviors.

SATIR'S MODEL OF INDIVIDUAL CHANGE

Our common reaction to change is to have a heightened stress level. Stress is not an undesirable aspect of a job, but it must be effectively managed. Stress that is above or below a certain comfort and motivational

Conflict Management and Leadership Development Using Mediation
pp. 1–3
Copyright © 2021 by Information Age Publishing

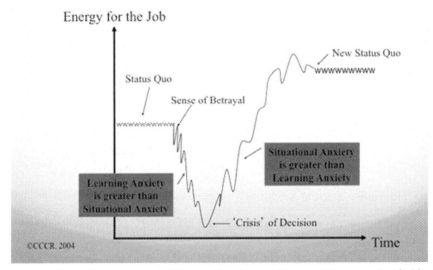

Source: Adapted from Satir et al. (1991) and by Algert and Watson (2005). Reprinted with permission.

Figure 1.1.   Satir's model for individuals and organizations.

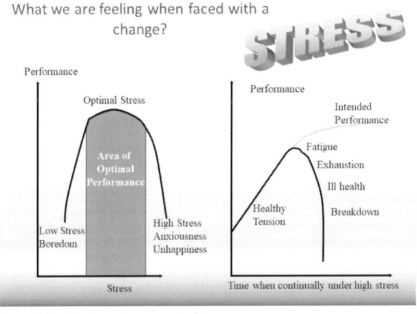

Figure 1.2.   Two important aspects of stress.

level will cause people to look for relief. We search for a resolution to the conflict (change) that causes the uncomfortable stress.

STRESS AND OUR PERFORMANCE

Stress is required for optimal performance, but long durations of time under stress eventually cause performance failure. Under distress or eustress, we move toward personal behavior patterns that we are most comfortable with, whether our behaviors are productive or counterproductive. Ironically, people often believe that their patterns of behavior are the obvious, rational, or expected behavior, rather than recognize the use of familiar patterns of behavior as coping habits.

In the workplace and at home, every individual consistently deals with complex combinations of changes and reactions generated by themselves, colleagues, and constituents with whom they interact. Conflicts will be a constant in the workplace due to these complexities.

CHAPTER 2

CONFLICT

> "We can often measure our progress by watching the nature of our conflicts.... If a man should tell you that his chief daily conflict within himself is "shall I steal or not steal?" you would know what to think of his development ... in the same way, one test of your [organization] is not how many conflicts do you have, for conflicts are the essence of life, but what are your conflicts, and how do you deal with them?"

—Mary Parker Follett (1920)

IMPORTANCE OF MANAGING CONFLICT

A conflict is a struggle or contest between people with opposing values, needs, ideas, beliefs, or goals. Conflict arises when the needs or interests of one person are perceived by that person as being denied to them by another. Conflict exists even if only one person acknowledges the struggle.

Typically, people react to conflict in one of two modes:

- flight from the situation; or
- fight to win.

Beyond the initial reaction to conflict, much more complex behavioral patterns will emerge. Common examples in the workplace would be to:

Conflict Management and Leadership Development Using Mediation
pp. 5–8
Copyright © 2021 by Information Age Publishing

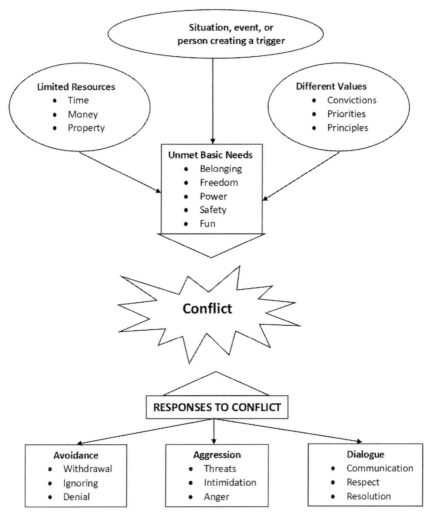

Figure 2.1.   Understanding how conflicts occur.

deny, argue, battle, compromise, collaborate, lie, cheat, help, give-in, hide, or avoid. Through development of conflict management skill sets, it is hoped that a third response to conflict becomes the norm, respectful commination and dialogue.

It is important to understand your own tendencies for addressing conflicts, especially because we tend to see our own behavior as the "right" behavior. In addition, if we can aid others in discerning conflict styles, rather than assuming people's intent, we may add valuable insight to management of the conflict.

CONFLICT MODES

Blake and Mouton (1964) created a framework that allows viewing of different conflict modes or types. The modes lie on a grid that compares the response to conflict by noting the levels of cooperation and assertiveness. The Thomas-Kilmann conflict mode instrument is based upon the Blake and Mouton grid. This is a self-report instrument that reflects the propensity of individuals to respond to conflict in one of five modes:

- competing;
- collaborating;
- compromising;
- avoiding; and
- accommodating.

The instrument is meant to show which style(s) an individual has the greatest tendency to use in a conflict. However, different conflicts and

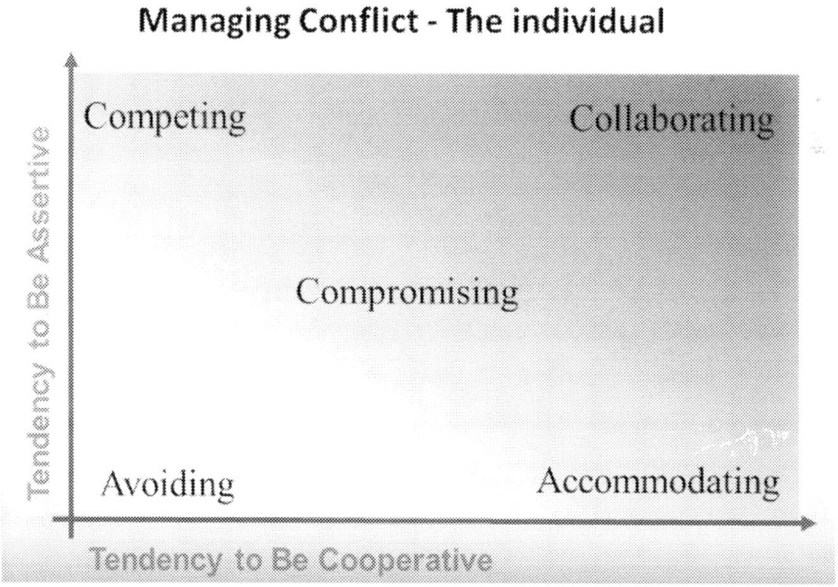

Managing Conflict - The individual

Figure 2.2.   The Thomas-Kilmann conflict mode instrument.

their surrounding factors will warrant different styles and each style can be deployed strategically. The more an individual understands each of the different styles, the more he/she may be able to choose the style most conducive for managing the conflict at hand.

For more detail, see https://www.cpp.com/products/tki/index.aspx

CONFLICT ESCALATION AND DEESCALATION

Unresolved conflict has the potential to cost an individual or organization significant time, energy, and resources, and can even lead to aggression or violence. Many believe that resolution of a conflict must traverse a path of de-escalation back through the stages that have been followed in escalation. See Table 2.1 for Thomas Jordan's summary of Glasl's model.

Table 2.1.   Conflict Escalation

	Stage	Conflict Issue	Behavioral Norms	Threshold to Next Level
1.	Hardening	Objective	Straight arguing	Tricks in argument
2.	Debate	Relative positioning	Verbal confrontation	One-sided action
3.	Action without words	Self-image	Symbolic behavior	Attacks aimed at other's identity
4.	Images and coalitions	Save reputation	Exploit gaps from coalition	Loss of face
5.	Loss of face	Fundamental values and dignity	Attack other publicly	Ultimatum or strength test
6.	Strategic threats	Control other	Ultimatums and binding statements	Execute ultimatum
7.	Limited "blows"	Hurt other survival	Attack other greater threats	Attack core of the enemy
8.	Shatter enemy	Annihilate other and survive	ATTACK on all levels	Sacrifice self-preservation
9.	Together into ABYSS	Annihilation at any cost	WAR limited violence	

Sources: Glasl (1982) and summarized by Jordan (2000).

CHAPTER 3

CONFLICT MANAGEMENT

WHAT IS ALTERNATIVE DISPUTE RESOLUTION?

The term "alternative dispute resolution" or ADR is often used to describe a wide variety of dispute resolution mechanisms that are short of, or alternatives to, full-scale court processes. The term can refer to everything from facilitated settlement negotiations, in which disputants are encouraged to negotiate directly with each other prior to some other legal process, to arbitration systems or minitrials that look and feel very much like a courtroom process. Processes designed to manage community tension or facilitate community development issues can also be included within the rubric of ADR. ADR systems may be categorized generally as negotiation, conciliation, mediation, or arbitration systems.

Negotiation systems create a structure to encourage and facilitate direct negotiation between parties to a dispute without the intervention of a third party. Mediation and conciliation systems are very similar in that they interject a third party between the disputants, either to mediate a specific dispute or to reconcile their relationship. Mediators and conciliators may simply facilitate communication, or may help direct and structure a settlement, but they do not have the authority to decide or rule on a settlement. Arbitration systems authorize a third party to decide how a dispute should be resolved.

It is important to distinguish between binding and nonbinding forms of ADR. Negotiation, mediation, and conciliation programs are nonbinding and depend on the willingness of the parties to reach a voluntary

Conflict Management and Leadership Development Using Mediation
pp. 9–16
Copyright © 2021 by Information Age Publishing

agreement. Arbitration programs may be either binding or nonbinding. Binding arbitration produces a third-party decision that the disputants must follow even if they disagree with the result, much like a judicial decision. Nonbinding arbitration produces a third-party decision that parties may reject.

It is also important to distinguish between mandatory processes and voluntary processes. Some judicial systems require litigants to negotiate, conciliate, mediate, or arbitrate prior to court action. ADR processes may also be required as part of a prior contractual agreement between parties. In voluntary processes, submission of a dispute to an ADR process depends entirely on the will of the parties.

The following information is extracted from the public information provided by the U.S. government describing recognized alternative dispute resolution methods in judicial practices: https://www.usaid.gov/sites/default/files/documents/1868/200sbe.pdf

A BRIEF HISTORY OF ADR[1]

Dispute resolution outside of courts is not new; societies all over the world have long used nonjudicial, indigenous methods to resolve conflicts. What is new is the extensive promotion and proliferation of ADR models, wider use of court-connected ADR, and the increasing use of ADR as a tool to realize goals broader than the settlement of specific disputes.

The ADR movement in the United States was launched in the 1970s, beginning as a social movement to resolve communitywide civil rights disputes through mediation and as a legal movement to address increased delay and expense in litigation arising from an overcrowded court system. The legal ADR movement in the United States has grown rapidly and has evolved from experimentation to institutionalization with the support of the American Bar Association, academics, courts, the U.S. Congress, and state governments. For example, in response to the 1990 Civil Justice Reform Act requiring all U.S. federal district courts to develop a plan to reduce cost and delay in civil litigation, most district courts have authorized or established some form of ADR. Innovations in ADR models, expansion of government-mandated, court-based ADR in state and federal systems, and increased interest in ADR by disputants has made the United States the richest source of experiences in court-connected ADR.

While the court-connected ADR movement flourished in the U.S. legal community, other ADR advocates saw the use of ADR methods outside the court system as a means to generate solutions to complex problems that would better meet the needs of disputants and their communities, reduce reliance on the legal system, strengthen local civic institutions, preserve disputants' relationships, and teach alternatives to violence or litigation for dispute settlement. In 1976, the San Francisco Community Boards program was established to further such goals. This experiment has spawned a variety of community-based ADR projects, such as school-based peer mediation programs and neighborhood justice centers.

In the 1980s, demand for ADR in the commercial sector began to grow as part of an effort to find more efficient and effective alternatives to litigation. Since this time, the use of private arbitration, mediation, and other forms of ADR in the business setting has risen dramatically, accompanied by an explosion in the number of private firms offering ADR services.

The move for experimentation to institutionalization in the ADR field has also affected U.S. administrative rule making and federal litigation practice. Laws now in place, authorize and encourage agencies to use negotiation and other forms of ADR in rule making, public consultation, and administrative dispute resolution.

Internationally, the ADR movement has also taken off in both developed and developing countries. ADR models may be straight-forward imports of processes found in the United States or hybrid experiments that mix ADR models with elements of traditional dispute resolution. ADR processes are being implemented to meet a wide range of social, legal, commercial, and political goals. In the developing world, a number of countries are engaging in the ADR experiment including Argentina, Bangladesh, Bolivia, Colombia, Ecuador, the Philippines, South Africa, Sri Lanka, Ukraine, and Uruguay. The experience of many of these countries provides important lessons.

THE CHARACTERISTICS OF ADR APPROACHES

Although the characteristics of negotiated settlement, conciliation, mediation, arbitration, and other forms of community justice vary, all share a few common elements of distinction from the formal judicial structure. These elements permit them to address development objectives in a manner that differentiates them from judicial systems.

1. *Informality*: Fundamentally, ADR processes are less formal than judicial processes. In most cases, the rules of procedure are flexible, without formal pleadings, extensive written documentation, or rules of evidence. This informality is appealing and important for increasing access to dispute resolution for parts of the population who may be intimidated by or unable to participate in more formal systems. It is also important for reducing the delay and cost of dis-

pute resolution. Most systems operate without formal representation.

2. *Application of Equity*: Equally important, ADR programs are instruments for the application of equity rather than the rule of law. Each case is decided by a third party or negotiated between disputants themselves based on principles and terms that seem equitable in the particular case, rather than on uniformly applied legal standards. ADR systems cannot be expected to establish legal precedents or implement changes in legal and social norms. ADR systems tend to achieve efficient settlements at the expense of consistent and uniform justice.

    In societies where large parts of the population do not receive any real measure of the overall system of justice, ADR can mitigate the problems by ensuring that disputants have recourse to formal legal protections if the result of the informal system is unfair and by monitoring the outcomes of the informal system to test for consistency and fairness.

3. *Direct Participation and Communication Between Disputants*: Other characteristics of ADR systems include more direct participation by the disputants in the process and design of settlements, more direct dialogue and opportunity for reconciliation between disputants, potentially higher levels of confidentiality because public records are not typically kept, more flexibility in designing creative settlements, less power to subpoena information, and less direct power of enforcement.

    Even in the United States, where ADR systems have been used and studied more extensively than in most developing countries, the impact of these characteristics is not clear. Many argue, however, that compliance and satisfaction with negotiated and mediated settlements exceed those measures for court-ordered decisions. The participation of disputants in the settlement decision, the opportunity for reconciliation, and the flexibility in settlement design seem to be important factors in the higher reported rates of compliance and satisfaction.

CHOOSING AN INTERVENTION APPROACH FOR CONFLICT

There are important considerations when choosing an approach to conflict intervention.

1. The long-term relations and interactions of the disputants with each other and with the intervening party.

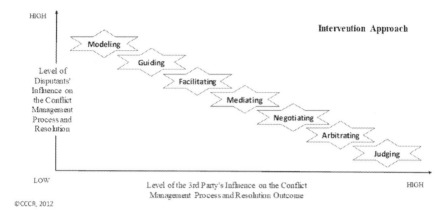

©CCCR, 2012

Source: Watson and Watson (2011). Reprinted with permission.

Figure 3.1. Styles of intervention management.

2. How much influence the disputants have in determining the process and resolution to the current conflict.
3. How much influence the intervening party has on the process and resolution.
4. How much effort, time and resources the approach will take.

Third parties' interveners should strategically choose a conflict mode that increases the likelihood they accomplish their desired goal. Examples of intervention strategies are listed below.

Modeling

Definition
- A person that serves as a pattern of behavior

Process/Tactic
- To be thoughtful and intentional in your workplace behavior

Skill Set
- Self-awareness to analyze your behavior
- Managing your emotions to model consistent behavior

Guiding

Definition

- To direct or supervise
- Guide implies intimate knowledge of the conflict and of all its difficulties and dangers

Process/Tactic

- Meet with disputant(s) to share, through experience, strategies and methods of conflict management that have worked for you

Skill Set

- Active listening to clarify information
- Perspective taking to understand disputants
- Sense of timing so employees believe you are supporting them

Facilitating

Definition

- To enter into an ongoing system of relationship for the purpose of helping the disputants

Process/Tactic

- To get disputants together to assist and support them in discussing and managing their conflict

Skill Set

- Active listening to understand issues and feelings
- Impartiality to fairly support disputants

Mediating

Definition

- Intervention into a dispute by an acceptable third party to assist disputing parties in voluntarily reaching their own mutually acceptable settlement of issues

Process/Tactic

- Get disputants together to discuss conflict, using a formal process to generate an agreement for conflict management

Skill Set

- Neutrality
- Nonthreatening confrontation to assist disputants in resolving conflict

Negotiating

Definition

- More directive than mediation
- Support disputants in negotiating a resolution to their conflict

Process/Tactic

- Bring disputants together to hear each other's issues and negotiate a compromise

Skill Set

- Analyzing input so parties can clearly decide resolution by assessing value of proposed solutions

Arbitrating

Definition

- Helping parties in controversy settle differences
- To render a decision

Process/Tactic

- Bring disputants together and determine the outcome of a dispute for disputing parties based upon information presented

Skill Set

- Decision-making to direct/determine outcome and/or consequence

Judging

Definition

- Appointment to decide outcome

Process/Tactic

- Meet with disputants to render a decision based upon information and the rules, policies, and procedures of an organization

Skill Set

- Awareness of policies to communicate to disputants
- Clear communication so disputants understand outcome

NOTE

1.   This history is drawn from a number of sources, including: Goldberg et al. (1992), and Elizabeth Plapinger and Donna Stienstra, ADR and Settlements in the Federal District Courts: A Sourcebook for Judges and Lawyers (Federal Judicial Center and CPR Institute for Dispute Resolution).

CHAPTER 4

CONFLICT ENGAGEMENT

The goal of conflict management is to have a "different kind of conversation" that involves self-reflection, mindfulness, and strategic thinking as illustrated in Figure 4.1.

Conflicts are managed and conversations are successful when the parties

- have the ability to be self-aware (e.g., identify hidden assumptions);
- are willing to and engage in self-awareness and self-reflection;
- frame the/their relationship;
- frame the conflict and the issue(s);
- practice mindfulness of one another;
- choose to exercise perspective taking;
- intentionally and strategically choose their conflict management mode(s);
- look for areas of common ground;
- move from positions to interests and needs;
- articulate what is wanted to accomplish desired end goal(s);
- articulate the desired end goal(s); and
- use an effective communication skill set.

When in conflict, people need to reflect on: (1) themselves and (2) others in the conflict.

Conflict Management and Leadership Development Using Mediation
pp. 17–27
Copyright © 2021 by Information Age Publishing
17

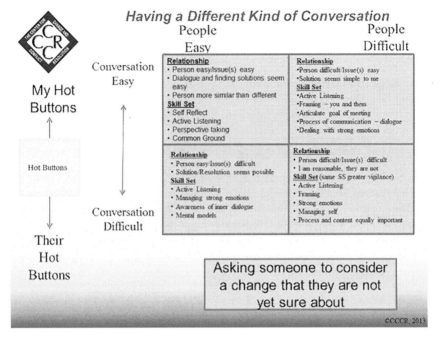

Figure 4.1.   Having a different kind of conversation.

Individuals in conflict situations should:

- identify the conflict and determine its impact on you;
- heighten awareness of how often you may be reacting to conflict and execute a conscious conflict management plan;
- observe how others appear to be reacting or responding to conflict;
- evaluate the styles/models of dealing with conflict being demonstrated by all;
- choose your style for managing the conflict;
- determine if intervention is wise and ask for it if appropriate; and
- be ready for the next conflict, but not hypervigilant.

Individuals intervening in others' conflict should:

- observe the behaviors surrounding the conflict and the consequences of these behaviors;
- identify the conflict by observation and by gathering input from disputants;

- review how you personally relate to the conflict given your current circumstances, and if your intervention is likely to be productive;
- review how you personally relate to the individuals in conflict, and if your intervention is likely to be productive and accepted;
- identify the nature of the conflict;
- determine your intervention goal;
- choose your intervention approach; and
- intervene, evaluate, and persevere, but not infinitely in the same mode.

IDENTIFYING THE CONFLICT

Conflicts are an important part of life. Although many people assume they are negative and, therefore, should be avoided, there are many positive outcomes experienced when a conflict is managed well. For example, most change is driven by some level of conflict. You must change to grow, to develop, to learn. Thus, the conflicts we deal with are essential to our development and our organizations' development. However, some conflicts escalate to the point that they can destroy individuals or organizations. The key to managing conflict is to understand and expect conflicts and manage them before they escalate into a destructive force.

There are two initial steps in identifying the conflict you may be faced with (1) recognize your physiological responses when perceiving conflict, and (2) notice and identify your thoughts and feelings.

For example, physiological conflict responses for some people entail sweaty palms, a shortness of breath or rapid breathing, stomach queasiness, headache, rapid eye movement, neck and shoulder tension, tingling sensation, lower back pain, and/or tightness in the jaw. When these signs are recognized, it should trigger self-awareness and the question, "Why is my body feeling this way?"

Thoughts and feelings people often have when in conflict are judgment, fear, guilt, anger, resentment, or they are doing it again, they are trying to win, they are messing with my area, I will not tolerate this, I do not like this, they are wrong. These kinds of thoughts often race through people's minds, bouncing back and forth from positive to negative thoughts in his/her mind.

In order to initiate appropriate management of a conflict, you must identify any feelings or thoughts that you have and understand that they indicate an unmet need.

DEVELOPING A CONFLICT MANAGEMENT PLAN

A conflict management plan is an invaluable tool in more effectively managing conflict individually and organizationally. Research shows that all people have a conflict management plan that is implemented when conflict is perceived; however, many of us are unaware of the plan we unconsciously act out.

We normally develop our conflict plan early in childhood; it happens at an unconscious level. The conflict plan most of us use as adults is what we saw modeled by our primary caregivers. Some had excellent adult models who taught effective conflict management. Others had adult role models who taught that conflict is bad and should be avoided at all cost. Some were even taught to "get others before they get us"—attack before someone attacks us. We carry these messages deep within us.

Unless we make a conscious choice to look at our unconscious conflict plan, we generally just react to conflict with our existing coping mechanisms. We continue to engage or ignore conflict consistent with our childhood molding. Those of us who were taught to fight, continue to fight anytime there is a conflict. Those of us who were taught to avoid and "pretend there is no conflict" continue to ignore the conflict. We practice what we unconsciously learned, and then are often unsatisfied with the outcome of our conflict engagement. While there is nothing inherently wrong with the conflict management you developed in childhood, it is often ineffective for the specific types of conflicts we are faced with later in life.

A conflict management plan is simply a set of sequential steps to follow when in conflict with another person. By consistently creating a conflict management plan, prior to being involved in a conflict, a person can: (1) thoughtfully create a productive intervention plan and (2) intentionally implement this plan when in conflict.

When Developing a Conflict Management Plan

- Decide that effectively managing conflict is important.
- Build a foundation of understanding about different conflict modes you can use to manage conflict.
- Refine and learn communication skills you view as essential to managing conflict.
- Determine your physiological indicators that will assist in determining if a conflict exists for you.
- Determine the physical, emotional, and cognitive experiences you have when in conflict.

- Determine if the conflict is yours personally or one you need to help others manage.
- Determine and write down specific steps you use (typically 4–8 steps) each time you are a part of the conflict.

To Effectively Use a Conflict Management Plan

- Use your plan each and every time you have a conflict.
- Review and modify your plan as you grow and change as a person.
- Review and modify your plan as your professional positions change.
- Adapt your plan to best support the conflict situation.
- Celebrate when you use your plan and see productive outcomes for you, others, and your organization.

It can be helpful to list four to eight steps that can be followed when you become aware of being in a conflict. Below is an illustration of a conflict management plan:

Conflict Management Plan Example

1. When I observe the following physiological responses, I will examine the thoughts surrounding them:

   - increased heart rate;
   - sweating;
   - knot in stomach; and/or
   - eyes dart about.

2. When I have the following feelings accompanying the physiological responses, I will examine the thoughts surrounding them:

   - anger;
   - judgment;
   - how do I escape from this person/situation?; and
   - they are trying to win!

3. Internal Responses

   - stop and do not flee* (initial reaction is to run from the conflict) *Some people's reaction is to fight rather than flight, and they too must manage whether to fight or not;

- breathe (helps me to relax and think before I speak);
- begin thinking and try to reduce my negative feelings (at times I'm too sensitive); and
- determine if the situation is my conflict and whether I need to address it.

4.   External Responses

- state my interest (not position) clearly;
- use active listening and I messages;
- respond thoughtfully;
- seek mutual understanding; and
- consider how we continue our personal or work relationship.

As you can see, the creation of a conflict management plan does not have to be a laborious process. The important point is to create it! By creating a plan, we can more thoughtfully respond to our conflicts and more often avoid reacting in a negative way. The following sections give more information so that you can best determine your general conflict plan and make specific plans for individuals with whom you may regularly be in conflict. Watch for a lack of accountability for the conflict. Individuals who always avoid a conflict are just as much to blame for conflict escalation as those who always engage. Defining a habitual reaction as "just who I am" is not a good conflict management strategy.

CONFLICT STYLES

As previously discussed, prior to developing specific skills, people typically deal with conflict in one of two ways:

- fight to win; there is always one or more losers; and
- flee from the situation.

In addition, individuals have a propensity to respond to conflict in on of five modes:

- competing;
- collaborating;
- compromising;
- avoiding; and
- accommodating.

The conflict style of an individual can be impacted by factors such as gender, self-concept or confidence, skill in dealing with conflicts, communication skills, and life experiences. Individuals in conflict will also choose styles to deal with the conflict that depend upon situational factors such as personal expectations and position or power. Conflict style is greatly influenced by the culture, both social and organizational, in which people operate. Numerous studies have documented differences, in general, in how men and women, or minorities and nonminorities handle conflicts in the United States. Learned behaviors in organizations, or units within the organization, often influence the styles chosen for managing conflicts. The key is to understand that these are learned behaviors and that they can be changed if desired.

People may choose a style in a given conflict situation depending upon personal and organizational norms, as well as upon the current escalation level of the conflict. Skill in managing conflict is demonstrated by choosing a style that will lead to deescalation of a conflict and, ultimately, a level of resolution that minimizes the resources and energy surrounding the issues in the conflict.

In all situations and with any style, some behaviors are assured to aid in conflict resolution:

- describe the other person's behavior objectively;
- use concrete terms;
- describe a specific time, place, and action of concern;
- describe the action, not the motive;
- acknowledge your feelings;
- express feelings as calmly as possible;
- use humor effectively;
- state feelings positively related to the goal;
- direct yourself to the specific behavior;
- ask for a change in the behavior;
- specify, if appropriate, what you are willing to change to make the agreement;
- reaffirm the other individual's ability to make a change; and
- end on a positive (not necessarily happy) note.

CHOOSING WHETHER TO ENGAGE IN A CONFLICT

There are times when we have a choice to avoid or engage in a conflict. The following six variables should be considered when deciding whether you will engage in a conflict:

1.   How invested in the relationship are you?

The importance of the working/personal relationship often dictates if you will engage in a conflict or not. If you value the person and/or the relationship, it is important to go through the process of conflict resolution.

2.   How important is the issue to you?

Even if the relationship is not of great value to you, one must often engage in conflict if the issue is personally important. For example, if the issue is a belief, value, or regulation that you believe in or are hired to enforce, then engaging in the conflict is necessary. If the relationship and the issue are important to you, then there is an even more compelling reason to engage in the conflict.

3.   Do you have energy for the conflict?

Many of us say, "There is not time to do all that I want to do in a day." We contend that more often than not, the issue is not how much time is available, but how much energy we have for what we need to do. Even in a track meet, runners are given recovery time before they have to run another race. It is the energy, not the time, being managed in these situations.

4.   Are you aware of the potential consequences?

Prior to engaging in a conflict, it is wise to think about anticipated consequences from engaging in the conflict. For example, there may be a safety risk, a risk of job loss, or an opportunity for a better working relationship. Many times people will engage in conflict and then be "shocked" by the outcome or consequences of engaging in the conflict. It is always useful to thoughtfully think through the consequences, whether positive or negative in nature.

5.   Are you ready for the consequences?

After identifying the potential consequences, you should determine if you are ready for the consequences of engaging in the conflict. For example, one employee anticipated a job loss if she continued to engage in the conflict she was having with her boss over a particular issue. After careful consideration, the employee thought and believed strongly enough about the issue that she did engage in the conflict with her boss. Her annual contract was not renewed for the upcoming year. Because this individual thought through the consequences of engaging in the conflict, she was prepared to be without a job for some time and able to financially and emotionally plan for this outcome. Most consequences of engaging in conflict are not this severe, but this example illustrates the value of thinking through consequences.

6.   What are the consequences if you do not engage in the conflict?

   Most people have values, ideas, beliefs, or morals that are a core part of their personhood. When a person is going to sacrifice one of his/her beliefs by not engaging in conflict, there is a concern of a personal loss of respect. Even if a person is not excited about the consequences of engaging in a conflict, he/she must also consider the consequences of not engaging in the conflict. When the personal consequences of not engaging in the conflict outweigh all other factors, then a person usually must engage in the conflict situation. At times, one must engage in conflict to not lose a sense of self.

NATURE OF CONFLICTS

Effectively framing conflict is important (Dewulf et al., 2009), and there are many ways and models to choose. What is most important for the conflict manager is to have an awareness of how we are framing the conflict and how each party in the conflict is framing the event. Typically, the parties in conflict have framed the conflict very differently from one another. Understanding everyone's framing helps the conflict manager support the parties in working to find common ground from which to address the conflict. Examples of framing models include:

1.   Relationship Conflicts
     Reason: Often about personal differences
     Intervention Techniques:
     - Manage emotions
     - Allow expressions of emotions
     - Clarify perceptions
     - Improve quantity and quality of dialogue/communication
     - Challenge negative behaviors
     - Encourage commitment to problem solving
2.   Data Conflicts
     Reason: Often an information deficiency
     Intervention Techniques:
     - Reach agreement on what data are important

  - Agree on a process to collect, communicate, and disseminate data
  - Use third-party experts to break deadlocks and get additional opinions

3. Interest Conflicts

   Reason: Often related to equity issues

   Intervention Techniques:

   - Focus on interests, not positions
   - Look for objective criteria
   - Develop integrative solutions that address the needs of all parties
   - Search for ways to expand options or resources
   - Develop trade-offs to satisfy interests of different strengths

4. Structural Conflicts

   Reason: Often environmental or personal stress

   Intervention Techniques:

   - Clearly define and change roles
   - Replace destructive behavior patterns
   - Reallocate ownership or control of resources
   - Establish a fair and mutually acceptable decision-making process
   - Change negotiation process from positional to interest-based bargaining

5. Value Conflicts

   Reason: Sometimes role incompatibility

   Intervention Techniques:

   - Avoid defining the problem in terms of value
   - Allow parties to disagree and agree
   - Create spheres of influence in which one set of values dominates
   - Search for a subordinate goal that all parties share

ESTABLISHING THE GOALS FOR YOUR INTERVENTION

In order to effectively address the conflict, it is important for the conflict manager to identify the goals for each individual in the conflict (including themselves) as well as the organizational goals.

Individuals

- an acceptable resolution of the specific conflict is reached;
- disputants' relationships are mended or strengthened;
- disputants' skills in conflict management are strengthened; and
- disputants' values or interests are adjusted.

Organization

- processes or procedures are changed;
- structure or composition of units or organization is changed;
- espoused values, interests or goals are changed;
- underlying values or assumptions are changed; and
- asking for third party intervention.

The next sections of this book will discuss conflicts in an organization, and present ideas for when and how people outside of a conflict should intervene in a conflict. Individual disputants should read these sections, as well, to understand when and what kind of intervention they may desire in a conflict situation.

CHAPTER 5

ORGANIZATIONAL CONFLICT

Recognize that an unresolved conflict has the potential to cost an organization significantly in time, resources, aggression, and violence. The reason an unresolved conflict becomes more costly is not only because of the potential for wasted resources in the midst of the conflict, but the need for resources to find a resolution typically increases as a conflict persists. This is often attributed to the escalation of the conflict.

EFFECTS OF UNRESOLVED CONFLICT

Often interveners do not plan for the actual goals they have for the outcomes of the intervention. This can result in choosing an intervention approach that is counterproductive for the actual goals of the intervention.

It is clear that if we improve our abilities to resolve conflicts, we will save resources, and we can also expect to see:

- improved understanding, even when parties remain in disagreement;
- improved communication; and
- improved productivity due to better utilization of resources and relationships.

It is clear that most conflicts that are typically ignored or mismanaged will escalate and become more costly to the organization. Recognizing

Conflict Management and Leadership Development Using Mediation
pp. 29–33
Copyright © 2021 by Information Age Publishing

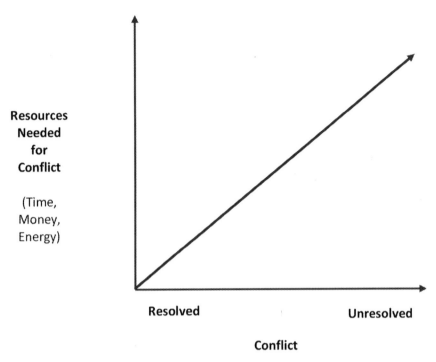

Figure 5.1.   Impact of unmanaged conflict.

how conflicts escalate will help someone understand how a conflict may be deescalated.

Research about conflicts shows that an unresolved conflict typically escalates; unresolved conflict can lead to aggression, which can lead to violence. Conflict is a high probability event; adults average five conflicts per day. Resolving conflict at its point of origin is the most beneficial approach.

It is valuable to address conflict at its point of origin for several reasons. First, when a conflict is addressed between the initial disputants/parties, the maximum number of options for resolution exists. As a conflict is "passed up through the ranks," the range of resolution options diminishes, and the options often are more punitive in nature. Second, it is empowering for the disputants to resolve their own conflicts versus having a hierarchical third party mandate the resolution. Through this empowerment, employees are more likely to follow through on their agreed upon resolution. Third, it is cost effective for conflicts to be resolved at their points of origin. As more parties become involved in resolving or managing conflict, each of these employees must spend more time away from their work responsibilities. Putnam reports that many people in management positions spend as much as 40% of their time managing and resolving conflicts.

Therefore, we advocate the value of teaching all employees conflict management skills. Most people do not resolve conflicts because they either have an unhoned skill set and/or because they do not know the organization's policy on conflict management. It is valuable for all employees to know their conflict styles, conflict intervention methods, strategies for conflict skill improvement, and the organization's support system for conflict management.

Often, after a conflict has escalated, well-meaning individuals believe that a simple choice by the disputants will refocus them on the original issues in the conflict. This results in interveners often getting pulled into one side or the other of the conflict. People typically must deescalate a conflict through the same, although hopefully abbreviated, stages they have escalated through.

DECIDING WHEN TO INTERVENE

People often think that conflict is "random"; it just occurs. Actually, the basis of conflict, related to unmet needs, is understandable and nonrandom. Being strategic in choosing to intervene and how to intervene is constructive.

TIPS FOR CONFLICT ENGAGEMENT

As a review of global concepts for conflict management, remember to:

1. Know yourself—be self-aware and engage in self-reflection.
2. Get to know others—know that others operate from a mental model (see references for more information) different than yours. Know that others think differently than you.
3. Understand different intervention strategies.
4. Have multiple communication and conflict management tools—a subset of some of the important conflict management skill sets are listed below. Use these skill sets for more effective conflict engagement:

    - Active listening
    - I statements/messages
    - Differing positions versus interests/needs

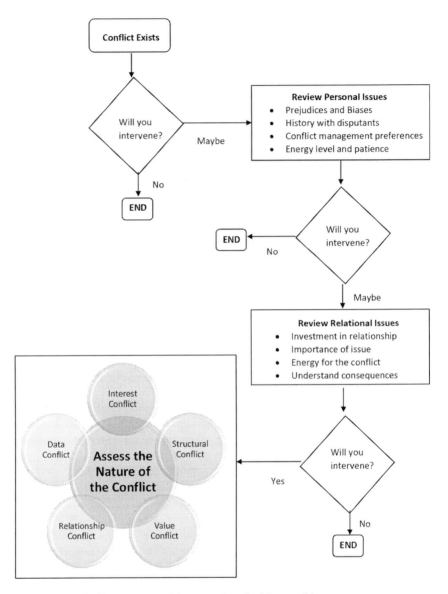

Figure 5.2. Guide to personal intervention decision-making.

5.   Avoid:

   - Using words like "you" and "why"—words such as why and you often put others on the defensive. Instead use language such as "help me to understand," "I am curious about your perspective," and describing your thoughts and feelings related to someone's behavior instead of saying something like "you made me mad."
   - The Drama Triangle—Karpman created the Drama Triangle which explains how conflicts can escalate and communication can diminish.

6.   Know how conflicts get managed/resolved—self-awareness and reflection, have a desired outcome, identify common ground, take perspective.

7.   Practice—start simple; engage in small conflicts to develop your skills.

8.   Care enough to engage—whether about you, someone else, the issue—and know the consequences of not engaging.

9.   Be honest—don't lie.

   - Say what you mean
   - Do not work to manipulate another person

10.   Know that conflict is—it simply is.

   - Conflicts exist and always will
   - Conflict is not a "bad thing"
   - Well-managed conflict can be positive, both personally and for the organization.

CHAPTER 6

MEDIATION

WHAT NECESSITATES A MEDIATION PROCESS?

The mediation process can be useful in supporting countless human interactions, but two major categories can often be identified: the need to change a basic pattern in a relationship or the need to solve a problem in the relationship. In reality, most mediations have varying combinations of these two categories. See Table 6.1.

PRINCIPLES OF MEDIATION

1. The desired outcome is two winners rather than one winner and one loser, or two losers.
2. To have two winners, there must be cooperation instead of competition.
3. To truly cooperate, the parties must have equal power in the mediation, regardless of any other status that they may have in their relationship.
4. While the past must be mutually understood, even if not agreed upon by all parties, the future is the primary focus.
5. To focus on the future, concentration must be on the interests and needs of the parties and not their current positions.
6. To truly understand needs, we must not only consider the facts and thoughts the parties can share, we must also consider their feelings and emotions.

Conflict Management and Leadership Development Using Mediation
pp. 35–51
Copyright © 2021 by Information Age Publishing

**Table 6.1.   Description of Two Categories of Conflict
That May be Supported by Mediation**

Change in Basic Pattern	*Solve a Problem*
• Identify the basic pattern	• Identify the problem
• Describe the characteristics of the basic pattern	• Describe the drivers that cause the problem
• Focus on parties' responsibility for characteristics	• Discern controllable, influential, and unchangeable drivers
• Discuss expected resistance to change	• Discuss realistic constraints on solutions
• Generate descriptions of desired basic patterns	• Generate possible solutions
• Discuss the changes required for the desired basic pattern	• Evaluate the trade-offs for the various solutions
• Plan steps that "unfreeze" resistance to change	• Analyze the quality of the solutions
• Plan steps that create momentum for desired change	• Select a solution
• Plan steps for making the change permanent	• Write an agreement that describes the solution to the problem

7. An environment where facts, thoughts, feelings and emotions are to be shared must be based on openness and honesty.

8. To trust that this kind of environment is possible, the parties must choose to be positive rather than negative about the prospects of success.

9. Therefore, mediation must be a voluntary experience, not a mandated one.

10. The outcome must be a mutually agreed upon solution, not an order by which all must abide.

11. The mediators follow established ethical guidelines (see Appendix 1).

THE MEDIATION PROCESS

The act of bringing a group of people together to work toward a common goal is the basic definition of a team. In a mediation situation, the disputants and mediator have a common goal of developing a resolution, or at least a management plan, to address a common problem for the disputants. Thus, in the mediation process, the participants must become a

Stages of Effective Teaming

Source: Tuckman (1965). Reprinted with permission.

Figure 6.1.   Tuckman's model of group interaction.

team. It is important to recognize that a set of team members do not have to like each other. Rather, they must acknowledge and value all members of the team, stay focused on the goals, and stay with the team process (plays or plans) so that the required interdependence of the team is used for progress instead of interference.

The mediator can benefit from understanding some basics concerning how effective teams normally progress together. From Scholters et al. (2003), we acknowledge that, often, we must appear to move away from good performance in order to set up the team dynamics that will foster positive performance in the long run.

STAGES OF THE MEDIATION PROCESS

Mediation is a multistage process. It is important to remember that the process is flexible. The mediator must use flexibility in controlling the stages of mediation so that a suitable resolution is found. Rigidity through

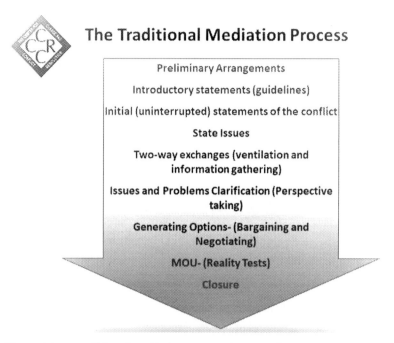

Figure 6.2. Traditional mediation process framework.

the stages of the process can doom a mediation. However, each stage has important aspects that lay the groundwork for future stages.

The mediation process is aligned with Tuckman's models of teams. The initial stages of mediation are forming, followed by the next stages of storming, generating options is norming, the memorandum of understanding (MOU), and the plan for their future relationship is performing.

MEDIATION PROCESS OUTLINE

1. *Preliminary Arrangements:* In this stage, the disputants agree to mediation and upon a mediator (or mediators), time, place, et cetera. When strong emotions are involved in the conflict, it is often useful for the mediator to have interviews with the disputants individually. In these interviews, the mediator strives to understand the needs and interests, as well as the position of the disputant, and provide coaching on acceptable conduct during the mediation sessions.

2. *Introductory Statements:* This marks the opening of the mediation session and, even if presented before, the roles and rules are pre-

sented to the disputants for them to agree to in the presence of each other.

3. *Initial Statements:* Each disputant has an uninterrupted opportunity to state his/her 'story' of the dispute. The order of presentation is determined during the introductory statement stage.

4. *Two-Way Exchanges:* The mediator helps the disputants share feelings and understand each other's viewpoints.

5. *Issues and Problems Clarification:* The mediator helps the disputants understand each other's needs and interests. The disputants clarify the issues and problems that prevent both parties' needs and interests from being met.

6. *Generating Options and Finding a Solution:* Disputants generate possible actions that will resolve the problems that are preventing the disputants' needs and interests from being met. The disputants agree upon a course of action to resolve the conflict.

7. *MOU Writing:* This stage involves laying out the solution in detail to assure that it can be implemented realistically and will potentially resolve the conflict.

8. *Closure:* The mediator affirms the disputants and closes the mediation process.

GOALS FOR EACH STAGE OF THE MEDIATION PROCESS

1. Introductory Statement (Mediator very active):

    • mediator establishes expectations for parties in conflict and what they can expect from mediators;

    • rapport building between comediators, mediators and parties in conflict (disputants), and the disputants where possible;

    • mediator explains process;

    • mediator works to increase self-awareness, encourages and models active listening, and works to reduce fears, stress, and concerns of disputants;

    • all, at the mediation table, are reminded that their needs, ideas, beliefs, values and goals will be heard; and

    • disputants share statements with other party that have not been heard before, explaining their perspective, their reasoning and responses, again, even if disputants are still in disagreement.

2. Two-Way Exchange (Mediator very active):

- disputants empowered to operate in the process and control aspects of the process;
- they take turns;
- they engage as active listeners;
- disputants vent issues they believe drove them to the current positions;
- disputants expose minor issues that may be triggering strong responses. If these issues are truly minor, they can be acknowledged as understandable and left or linked appropriately with the major issues;
- mediator notes and exposes patterns of behavior that lack cooperation including avoidance in the form of spin-offs, dead ends, diversions and competition in the form of blaming, hurting, pulling on mediator to be on their side;
- disputants focus on norming (agreeing) when possible;
- mediator uses what he/she sees, hears, and feels in order to translate for other party;
- everyone is listening/looking for commonalities;
- disputants begin to focus on major or priority issues that need resolution;
- mediator notes and has disputants acknowledge differences between the two parties;
- mediator helps disputants find emerging win-win outcomes;
- mediator looks for ways to help parties save face; and
- mediator begins to focus disputants on interests and needs rather than positions.

3. Formulation of Issues and Clarification:

- disputants make issues sharp and focused;
- mediator forces parties to focus on major issues, rather than every incident;
- mediator reinforces interdependences by pushing parties to understand and validate other's perspectives; and
- mediator clarifies the differences that still cause unmet needs for the disputants.

4.   Option Generating and Finding Solutions

- mediator structures the process, so options are generated before they are evaluated;
- disputants describe details of the options they propose;
- mediator formulates questions to pull option details out and cause more options to be generated;
- mediator directs the disputants toward patterns of behavior that incorporate cooperation;
- disputants collaborate to generate new options that allow optimal trade-offs for all parties;
- disputants compromise so that there is balance of wins and losses for all parties;
- disputants accommodate on issues that have less of a priority for them than the issues have for the other;
- everyone evaluates and reconciles the options, which may include linking issues or breaking them down into smaller pieces; and
- disputants agree on options for settlement.

5.   Writing and Reality Testing of MOU:

- mediator pushes disputants to test long-term reality of agreement by asking questions, "What if …";
- mediator asks tough questions regarding who, what, when, where, how;
- disputants think of any remaining issues not brought out;
- mediator exposes and clears up hidden agendas;
- mediator checks with disputants to make sure the MOU is realistic, specific, and balanced;
- mediator writes a MOU in terms agreed to by both parties (each sentence ~ 7–10 words); and
- mediator assures significant details of solution are captured in the MOU (dot Is and cross Ts).

6.   Closure

- Mediator affirms good work to help agreement to close
- Mediator closes the mediation with instructions and descriptions of follow-up action

MEDIATION TOOLKIT: MEDIATION PROCESS SCRIPTS

Preliminary Arrangements: Getting Ready

Meeting Separately with Disputants (Optional)

Use this step to begin the mediation when disputants have strong feelings.

Purpose:

- mediators meet separately with the disputants when there is high emotion such as anger;
- mediators allow disputants to vent emotions and/or anger about the situation;
- review mediation process and make sure that parties understand what will be happening;
- review your role as the mediator;
- begin to develop rapport with parties and trust in mediators and process; and
- review and get agreement to mediate and guidelines for behavior.

Procedures:

1. Mediators meet separately with each of the disputants for a short meeting (10–15 min. or longer if necessary).

2. Introduce yourselves and explain the role of the mediators.

   M: My name is _____ and I am a mediator.

   M: I am here to support you in a process to assist you in solving your problem with _____.

   or

   M: (name of other disputant) wants to solve his/her problem with you I am here to support you through the process of mediation.

   M: Mediation is voluntary. We have no power to make a decision for you. We will not take sides or decide who is right or wrong.

3. Explain the mediation process.

   M: Mediation is a process in which we help you talk about the problem, look for possible solutions, and get a MOU that you both feel is fair.

M: Everything that is said here is confidential, except for a few things (homicide, suicide, and abuse) and issues related to harassment.

4.   Ask each disputant to tell his/her story/narrative.

M: Tell me what happened and how you are feeling about it.

Repeat using your own words to summarize what was said and how they are feeling about it.

5.   Get agreement to mediate.

M: Are you ready to try to solve your conflict in mediation?

If they say yes, they are ready, prepare for the mediation. If they say no, ask them what they need in order to begin. Below are suggestions for helping the disputants agree to mediation if they are hesitant about mediating.

M: What do you need in order to solve this conflict?

M: What would you like to get out of mediation?

 Find out what alternatives they have if they don't mediate.

M: What will happen if you don't solve the conflict in mediation?

Identify some of the advantages of mediation.

M: You will have a chance to express your feelings and point of view.

M: You will be able to talk about the conflict in a safe and neutral place.

M: You will be able to work towards a resolution to the conflict that is fair to both of you.

M: It's a chance to improve the situation rather than making it worse.

6.   Explain the guidelines for behavior (Rules).

M: In order for mediation to work, we need you to agree to some rules for behavior:

- no name calling or put-downs;
- no interrupting when someone is talking;

- be as honest as you can;
- no physical fighting or threats; and
- agree to try to solve the problem.

7. Ask if there are any questions.

8. Explain when and where the mediation will take place.

Introductory Statements: Roles and Rules

Purpose:

- review mediation process and make sure that parties understand what will be happening;
- review your role as mediator;
- begin to develop rapport with parties and trust in mediators and process; and
- review and get agreement to mediate and guidelines for behavior.

Procedures:

1. Roles: Introduce yourselves and tell the role of the mediators.

    M: Hi, my name is _____, and this is _____, we are your mediators.

    M: We are here to support you two in a process that may assist you in solving your problem/conflict.

    M: Mediation is voluntary. We will not decide who is right or wrong, take sides, or make decisions for you.

    M: Each of you will have a chance to discuss ways of solving your problem so each of you gets what you need.

    M: A MOU will be written and signed.

    M: Everything that is said in here is confidential, except for a few things (homicide, suicide, and abuse) and harassment and discrimination.

2. Rules: Explain to get agreement to guidelines for behavior.

    M: For mediation to work, we need you to agree to these rules:

    - no name-calling or put-downs;
    - no interrupting when someone is talking (here is some paper);

- be as honest as you can;
- no physical fights or threats;
- agree to try to solve the problem;
- speak directly to us at first, if necessary;
- clarify any time constraints;
- comfortable with us as mediators?; and
- no electronic recordings, this is not discovery.

3. Ask if there are any questions.

Initial Statements

Purpose:

- To allow parties to describe their view of the situation (tell their story) and express feelings.

Procedures:

1. Decide who will talk first. Ask the first person to describe how they see the situation and how they are feeling about it. Get the *facts* and *feelings* behind each issue.

   M: (name), could you tell us about the problem (what happened) and how you feel about it?

   Restate the facts and feelings using your own words.

2. Ask the second person to tell how they see the situation and how they are feeling about it.

   M: (name), could you tell us about the problem (what happened) and how you feel about it?

   Restate the facts and feelings using your own words.

Two-Way Exchanges

Purpose:

- To allow participants to begin to actively listen, see other perspectives, and gain new understanding.

Procedures:

1.   Ask person #1 if he/she will respond to what the other side said.

     M: (name), would you respond to what (name) said?

     Restate each response using Active Listening.

2.   Ask person #2 if he/she will respond to what the other side said.

     M: (name), please respond to what (name) said.

     Restate each response using active listening.

3.   Optional: Ask questions of each disputant to help clarify and to get more information. Possible questions:

     M: Can you tell us more about (name)?

     M: How long have you two known each other?

     M: How long has this problem been going on?

     M: Where or when did this happen?

     Use good teamwork if there are co-mediators.

Issues and Problems Clarification

Purpose:

•   Mediators help parties to understand each other's point of view. (Understanding does not mean agreement).

Procedures:

1.   Ask parties to summarize each other's point of view and feelings about the problem. (Facts and feelings)

     M: (name), would you tell us what you heard (name) say about this problem and how she/he is feeling about it?

2.   Ask the other person if the summary was correct.

M: (name), is that correct?

If the person misunderstood or didn't get all the facts and feelings, ask the other person to say it again.

3.   Repeat Step 1 with the other party asked to speak.

4.   Repeat Step 2 with the other person speaking.

Summarize all the facts and feelings as each person said them.

Find the things they have in common. For example:

M: (name), we heard you say that (names) used to be your friend, but it makes you angry when she/he talks with your boyfriend. Is that right?

M: (name), we heard you say that you don't like it when (name) talks about you to your neighbor. You feel angry when (name) doesn't say things straight to you. Is that right?

or

M: We heard you both say that you used to be friends but now you are both angry and upset because of a problem about something that you both heard. Is that correct?

5.   Identify *issues* and look for *common ground*.

6.   Make sure that both persons have said everything that they need to say.

M: Is there anything else that either of you needs to say before we go on to the next part?

Generating Options and Finding a Solution

Purpose:

- To "brainstorm" ideas to find a fair solution to the problem.
- To encourage the parties to cooperate in order to find a solution that is one to which they both can agree.
- To help the parties evaluate the possible solution in order to get a workable agreement.

Procedures:

1. Explain that you will now support them as they find a solution to their problem.

    M: We will now talk about a solution to the problem that you will both feel is fair and one that you can live with.

2. Ask the first person what he/she thinks is a fair solution to the problem.

    M: What do you think is a fair solution to the problem?

    or

    M: What do you need in order to solve this problem?

    Encourage them to come up with their own solutions. If they have difficulty thinking of something, you can say:

    M: If this problem happened again, what would you do differently to prevent it?

    If they still cannot think of a solution to the problem, remind them that they agreed to try and solve the problem. Only offer choices if necessary, for example,

    M: In a similar situation, the people decided to...

    M: If (name) were willing to... what would you be willing to do?

3. Restate what the person needs in order to solve the problem. Encourage each person to come up with more than one idea. Do not allow the other party to judge the possible solutions.

4. Ask the second party what she/he thinks is a fair solution to the problem.

    M: What do you think is a fair solution to the problem?

    or

    M: What do you need in order to solve this problem?

Encourage them to come up with their own solutions. If they have difficulty thinking of something, you can say:

M: If this problem happened again, what would you do differently to prevent it?

If they still cannot think of a solution to the problem remind them that they agreed to try and solve the problem. Only offer choices if necessary, such as,

M: In a similar situation, the people decided to …

M: If (name) were willing to … what would you be willing to do?

5.   Help the parties find a solution they can both agree to.

6.   Help the parties evaluate the solutions to make sure that they are:

   • Realistic (it can be done)
   • Specific (defines what, where, when, who, how)
   • Balanced (both parties are part of the agreement)

7.   Summarize and restate all parts of the agreement. Check with the parties to make sure that it is accurate.

Writing the Memorandum of Understanding

Purpose:

   • To write a MOU that states, in their language, all the issues and concerns defined by the parties.
   • To determine if the MOU needs to be reviewed or evaluated after a trial period of time.
   • To clearly define how the MOU will be carried out.

Procedures:

1.   Write the MOU on a mediation report form.

2.   Read the MOU and allow the parties to make changes if necessary.

3.   Have each party sign the MOU.

M: This MOU is a record of what each of you agrees to and shows that you are serious about resolving this dispute.

Closure

Purpose:

- Provide closure to the session and affirm work of the disputants in resolving the conflict.

Procedures:

1. Ask the parties if they need to meet again to review the MOU. Ask parties if they are going to work with others (e.g. attorney in civil mediation) on the MOU.

2. Ask the parties if they are willing to come back to mediation first if their MOU breaks down.

3. (If appropriate) remind the parties about rumors. Ask them to tell their friends, families and neighbors that their conflict has been resolved.

    M: To keep rumors from spreading, would you agree to tell your friends, families, and neighbors that your conflict is resolved?

4. Congratulate them for their hard work and for reaching an agreement.

    M: Congratulations on working hard for resolution of your conflict.

    Go over the process as many times as needed.

    Be sure to ask, "What if?" questions.

    Restate! Restate! Restate!

Example of Comediator Teamwork

Mediator #1—Opening: Roles

M: This is _____ and my name is _____. During the mediation you will both be given a chance to talk. We are not here to judge you or to take sides. We will not decide who is right or wrong or how you will solve your problem. When we finish you will come up with a memorandum of understanding and everything is confidential (explain when break confidentiality).

Mediator #2—Rules

M: You will both need to agree to some rules before we begin the mediation.

- no name-calling or put-downs;
- no interrupting when someone is talking;
- be as honest as you can;
- no physical fighting or threats;
- agree to try to solve the problem;
- speak directly to us at first, if necessary;
- questions?;
- comfortable with us as mediators;?
- no electronic recording of mediation; and
- time constraints.

Alternate inviting disputants to speak and restate what is heard. Continue alternating invitations to disputant to share and to clarify each other's positions. Continue alternating invitations for ideas and restatement of ideas during the generation of solutions.

Mediator #1—Agreement/MOU

Summarize solutions and get verbal agreement.

Mediator # 2—Agreement/MOU

Write solutions on agreement form.

A case study involved in creating the Multiparty Narrative Mediation (MNM) model and combined narrative is shared below.

CHAPTER 7

MODELS OF MEDIATION

All models assume we, as mediators, need to move the disputants higher on the cooperative axis from where they are initially presenting. Further, our goal is to keep all disputants assertive regarding their needs and interest so that one party is not accommodating on all issues. The assumption of all models is: (1) the disputants want to find a resolution and (2) their needs and interests can be met.

TRADITIONAL MEDIATION MODEL

In this model, there are a set of basic and process assumptions.

Basic Assumptions

1. The mediator(s) can assume a neutral state.
2. History is allowed to gain understanding of the conflict issues that are the focus of the mediation.
3. Narrowing the focus will enhance the chance of success.

Process Assumptions

1. Taking equal turns and disallowing abuse assures fairness.

Conflict Management and Leadership Development Using Mediation
pp. 53–75
Copyright © 2021 by Information Age Publishing

2.   Focusing should work to narrow the information presented to the conflict issues that need and can be resolved.

3.   Solution generation by the parties enhances buy in.

4.   Reality, specificity, and balance will ensure fairness.

MULTIPARTY NARRATIVE MEDIATION (MNM) MODEL

This model was developed as a variation to the traditional model and many find it a useful and practical method to use. It challenges both the basic and process assumptions of the traditional model.

Basic Assumptions

1.   Since no one can be absolutely neutral, the mediators must be very conscious of their own mental models concerning the disputants, the conflict, and the process.

2.   History must be used to help each disputant become more conscious of their mental models concerning the other party and the conflict.

3.   A narrow focus may help get a resolution, but it may not be the best resolution especially considering the ongoing relationship of the disputants.

Process Assumptions

1.   Statistically the party that gets to go first is unintentionally advantaged over 80% of the time; therefore, the mediators will strive to negate this advantage.

2.   Perspective taking, including awareness of the other persons 'reasonable' mental model, will enhance collaborative solution generation.

3.   Rather than the first turn in the mediation being one of the disputants, the mediators will first tell the history leading to the conflict based on the combined information of disputants placed on a chronological format, including factors that have contributed to each disputant's mental modeling. Equal turns will follow to explain, correct, or elaborate the history presented until each disputant believes an accurate history leading to the current status of the conflict is presented.

4. Focus should be on needs for resolution for the current conflict and on the on-going relationship of the disputants.

5. Specificity, reality, and balance are important in regard to the conflict as it fits in the context of on-going relationship.

The arrow illustration in Figure 7.1. shows what is being accomplished in the MNM model of obtaining the parties narratives.

EXAMPLE OF USING THE TWO MODELS

Jess, a White, female/male, professor, is in conflict with Stacy, an African American, female, associate professor, concerning the use of resources, specifically who will have a teacher assistant (TA) and who will not. The senior faculty member makes these assignments and has not given Stacy a TA for the semester, while another faculty member, Mike, a White, male, associate professor, has received a TA for his course.

Stacy is certain that Jess has used personal biases in making the assignment because when Mike taught the course Stacy is scheduled to teach, he was assigned a TA. Furthermore, his current course assignment has never had a TA assigned to it before. The issue is simply that Jess does not like or respect Stacy and uses every opportunity to impede her work.

Jess is certain that her/his TA assignments are fair considering the current resources available and the departmental history. The issue is fundamentally based on algorithms for enrollment numbers and innovations proposed, as well as consideration of faculty needs to break algorithmic ties if resources are too scarce to give everyone a TA.

TRADITIONAL MODEL BEGINNING

Mediators will decide to have either Jess or Stacy present their version of the issue first. If Stacy goes first, then Jess may spend a significant part of his/her time addressing the fact that he/she does not dislike Stacy, and that he/she has never impeded Stacy's work. If Jess goes first, Stacy may spend a significant part of her time addressing the facts surrounding the algorithm for TA assignments and why it appears to be unfair.

Preliminary Arrangements

Individual Stories with Mediators

Joint Clarification of "True" Stories

Synthesize Into One "True" Story

Issues and Problems Clarification

Generating Options (bargaining & negotiating)

Agreement Writing (reality tests)

Closure

Preliminary Arrangements
- Setting environment of trust and comfort with what will occur
- Understanding volunteers and commitments
- Agreeing to commitment and confidentiality

Individual Stories with Mediators
- Modeling an environment of active listening
- Establishing the appreciation and valuing of the story (Cloke)
- Mediators begin to work on self-neutralization and power neutralization for mediation (Wing)
- Mediators must gain permission from disputants for any material from the individual stories to be presented

Joint Clarification of "True" Stories
- Mediator's present aligned stories, looking for elements of commonality, neutral presentation, and exposure of actions, intents, beliefs, and feelings.
- Setting environment where disputants are not disempowered but are minimized in working hidden agendas (S, Hart, N. Kline, Bono – Six Hats). Let disputants' correct errors of what was presented or what was omitted now that they see aligned stories.
- See if the disputants can articulate what their story says about them – fundamental difference to traditional mediation model (storytelling, social justice literature, mental models, let D's tell us what sort means after they've heard our interpretation of stories). This may deepen the exposure of a disputant's mental model.

Synthesize into One "True" Story
- Setting environment for understanding we are weaving stories together not judging truth or value of stories.
- Integrate (go beyond the meaning of my story to the meaning of the stories for both) –
  - Can D1 understand, not necessarily agree with, D2 perspective and
  - What does other D's perspective mean to me

Issues and Problems Clarification
- What does the woven story reveal that needs to be resolved (what are the issues)
- Clarify issues so that we understand what is in conflict

Generating Options
- Brainstorm, non-judgmentally, creative options to resolve or minimize conflicts
- Bargain and negotiate which options are the most likely to be effective, efficient, achievable, controllable, desirable

MOU
- Realistic, specific, and balanced
- Where to disseminate

Figure 7.1.   Multiparty Narrative Mediation (MNM) model process framework.

MNM MODEL BEGINNING

After 45–60-minute interviews with each disputant, the mediators begin the mediation with the following:

	Stacy		Jess	
	Feelings	*Thoughts*	*Feelings*	*Thoughts*
2003			Excited to join the department, and nervous as the first woman/man	She/he was qualified but knew she/he had to make it like all the men/women; had to be respected
2012	Excited to join the department because they made her/him feel valued and respected. A bit nervous due to having the dimension of _____	Could contribute, make a difference, her/his passions aligned with institution's espoused values	Anger that the faculty were "ignored" as the normal recruiting process was not engaged to hire the first _____ diver member of the department	Diversity may have been overemphasized and possibly overrode other very important issues in the hiring of Stacy
2013	Hurt and angered by hostilities, devaluing, and being ignored by Jess and others in curricula meetings	This is not much fun, may get better after tenure, why won't others who agree with her/him speak up to counter Jess's opinions	Sad and angry because Mike almost did not get tenure because everyone compared him to Stacy	Stacy was given many more resources and opportunities than normal assistant professors because she/he is from a historically underrepresented group in the department
2014	Hurt and stressed by sharp criticisms about her/his work and teaching, it's like people are watching for every little mistake	I made it (tenure), maybe it gets better now—I can start doing other things to accomplish even more work in the field	Confused and disappointed that valued colleagues did not even analyze Stacy's promotion package like they normally do	Stacy's tenure is deserved but she/he certainly has no earned it like everyone else had to
2016	Current conflict—ignored, devalued, punished, not given same chances to contribute to the field	May need to leave, does not know how to connect so *they* understand her/him and her/his research. TA assignment is an indication of whether they value the time you need for research	Tired of Stacy thinking she/he deserves special treatment and concerned for the standards Jess and others have assured exist in the department. Sympathetic	Stacy has been treated fairly, it is her/his turn to think about the department and make some sacrifices for others/ it's for her/his own good.

MEDIATOR SKILL CHECKLIST

	Needs More Work			Mastered Skill	
Personal and Communication Skills					
1. Active Listening: attention to verbal and nonverbal cues	1	2	3	4	5
2. Using clear language	1	2	3	4	5
3. Asking neutral questions	1	2	3	4	5
4. Remaining patient	1	2	3	4	5
5. Remaining neutral	1	2	3	4	5
6. Working as a team	1	2	3	4	5
Roles and Rules: Setting the Stage					
1. Explaining the role of the mediator	1	2	3	4	5
2. Explaining the mediation process	1	2	3	4	5
3. Creating a comfortable place for mediation to happen	1	2	3	4	5
4. Establishing rapport	1	2	3	4	5
Facts and Feelings: Defining the Problem					
1. Listening/note-taking skills	1	2	3	4	5
2. Ability to be objective and non-judgmental	1	2	3	4	5
3. Using active listening	1	2	3	4	5
4. Clarifying issues	1	2	3	4	5
Finding Solutions					
1. Using active listening	1	2	3	4	5
2. Getting ideas for resolution	1	2	3	4	5
3. Using reality testing	1	2	3	4	5
4. Ability to summarize and write an agreement	1	2	3	4	5
5. Congratulating the disputants	1	2	3	4	5

SKILL SET REFINEMENT

Use the following worksheets and examples to hone skill sets that are important in the mediation and conflict management process.

ACTIVE LISTENING WORKSHEET

Techniques for Active Listening

1. Encourage the other person to keep talking. Show that you are interested in what they are saying. Use open-ended questions. Example: "Can you tell us more?"

2. Ask questions to get more information or to better understand the problem. Example: "Where did this happen?" "How long have you known each other?"

3. Restate in your own words the basic ideas—facts and feelings. Example: "So you were in the parking lot and he tripped you and you're feeling angry."

4. Summarize the important ideas and feelings as each person said them. Identify the things they have in common. Example: "This seems to be what happened ... and you're feeling (or you're both feeling) ... Is that right?"

The following are examples of things that might be said in a mediation. In each of the examples that follow, write down possible questions or statements that you might say as mediator.

Encouraging

- Disputant: She's always taking things of mine without asking permission. I don't know, I'm just angry at her because taking my report was the last straw.
- What would you say to encourage this person to keep talking?

_____

_____

_____

_____

Questioning

- Disputant: "My boss is always blaming me for everything. It doesn't matter whether I speak up in a meeting or not. She thinks I'm the one who does it."
- What questions could you ask to get more information or to understand the problem better?

_____

_____

_____

_____

Restating

- Disputant: "Sometimes Dr. Imbrie talks very fast, and I have a hard time understanding what he says. But I'm afraid to ask him to repeat himself. I'm afraid he will get mad at me."
- How can you restate these ideas and feelings?

_____

_____

_____

_____

Summarizing

- Disputant: "She was spreading rumors that I was talking to her boyfriend and trying to influence his opinion, but that's not true at all. It was her boyfriend who came up to me in the cafeteria and started talking. She's making a big thing out of nothing."
- What important ideas and feelings can you summarize from what was said?

_____

_____

_____

_____

LISTENING DOS AND DON'TS

Dos	Don'ts
• Focus attention on speaker	• Talk about yourself, be critical or give advice
• Repeat back in your own words	• Only say "mmm," "ah hah," or parrot their words
• Restate important thoughts and feelings	• Ignore the facts and feelings
• Reflect back so that they can hear and understand themselves	• Pretend that you understand or assume that you know it all
• Ask questions to make it clearer or to get more information	• Be a poor listener with your voice, eyes, and body
• Show listening with your voice, eyes, and body	• Fill every space with your talk
• Summarize facts and feelings	• Fix, change, or improve what they said
• Stay neutral	• Take sides

LISTENING FOR FEELINGS WORKSHEET

Change these "thought" statements to "feeling" statements. Use our listening for feelings worksheet for possible feelings/emotions.

Example:

- Thought statement: "What a drag, there's nothing to do."
- Feeling Statement: "It sounds like you're bored."

Suggestions for possible ways to begin a "feeling statement":

- It sounds like you're feeling ...
- It seems that you're feeling ...
- What I hear you saying is that you're feeling ...

1. Thought statement: "You never yell at him, always me."

    - Feeling statement:

      _____

      _____

      _____

      _____

2. Thought statement: "I don't need your help. I can do this myself."

    - Feeling statement:

      _____

      _____

      _____

      _____

3. Thought statement: "I can't believe it. I got a pay raise."

    - Feeling statement:

      _____

      _____

      _____

      _____

4. Thought statement: "Every time she says that I feel like punching her out."

    • Feeling statement:

    _____
    _____
    _____
    _____

5. Thought statement: "How's my performance? Do you think I'll get a good evaluation?"

    • Feeling statement:

    _____
    _____
    _____
    _____

6. Thought statement: "Leave me alone. Nobody cares about me anyway."

    • Feeling statement:

    _____
    _____
    _____
    _____

7. Thought statement: "You narc! You'd turn in your own brother."

    • Feeling statement:

    _____
    _____
    _____
    _____

8. Thought statement: "I feel like dancing when I hear that song."

    • Feeling statement:

    _____
    _____
    _____
    _____

FEELINGS VOCABULARY

Verbal messages in a conflict have facts and feelings. Mediators must be able to respond to both the content or facts and the feelings of the disputants.

Following is a list of words that describe feelings. The list may be helpful in identifying feelings and forming active listening responses.

Concerned	Attacked	Surprised
Confused	Ignored	Scared
Angry	Upset	Blamed
Frustrated	Embarrassed	Hateful
Annoyed	Hurt	Delighted
Put Down	Uncomfortable	Great
Misunderstood	Ripped-off	Betrayed
Worried	Disappointed	Irritated
Proud	Left Out	Important
_____	_____	_____
_____	_____	_____
_____	_____	_____
_____	_____	_____
_____	_____	_____
_____	_____	_____
_____	_____	_____

ANGER WORKSHEET

In a small group, discuss the following questions with one another:

1.   How do I act wen I'm angry?

_____
_____
_____
_____

2.   How do I react/feel when someone else is angry?

_____
_____
_____
_____

After discussion of #1 and #2, identify (as a group) those communication skills or techniques that would be helpful for a mediator to use in defusing anger. Assign a recorder who will report your ideas into the large group at the end of the discussion.

_____

_____

_____

_____

BLOCKS TO CREATIVE PROBLEM SOLVING

Mediators work to allow disputants to have a safe and constructive environment for creative problem solving. Creativity is the act of originating or bringing about a suggestion, plan, solution, an idea that is characterized by its originality, uniqueness, or imaginativeness. Creativity is enhanced when one is not overly critical of the ideas that are passing through their thoughts. Many things can impede creativity, including thoughts like:

- there can only be one right answer;
- that is not a logical idea;
- follow the rules, which are usually "my rules";
- be practical in your thinking;
- avoid ambiguity;
- to err is wrong; say nothing instead of being wrong;
- play is frivolous;
- that is not my area of expertise;
- do not be foolish; and
- I am not a creative person.

BODY LANGUAGE

Humans communicate in a variety of ways. They not only speak to get their messages across, but they use their bodies to give signals too. Bodies communicate with a diverse vocabulary of gestures, postures, eye movements, twitches, grimaces, and stares. Sometimes, what the body says is a lot closer to reality than what the voice says, which is why being able to recognize and interpret body signals is a valuable asset. You might call it "tuning in to the vibes." Some people are able to respond unconsciously to body language without quite knowing why or how. Be a good observer!

Body language can tell us a lot about what someone is feeling. It is useful information to have on hand when observing disputants. As a mediator, it is important not only to read other people's body language, but to also be conscious of your own body language. With the right gestures or movements, you can control many situations without seeming to be intentionally doing so. Body language can convey neutrality, confidence, and empathy, all important skills for mediations.

- Make eye contact.
- Nod head to affirm the speaker.
- Lean body forward slightly toward speaker.
- Keep arms unfolded.
- Use appropriate facial expressions to show interest and attention (Klose & Olivares, 1999).

I STATEMENTS

I statements are the process by which:

- we construct messages that convey accurate information about our feelings and content; and
- we speak so others may listen and respond in an empathetic or rational way.

Purpose:

- to make a clear, clean statement of your experience of an event, incident, et cetera, in a way that another person will hear and not need to defend.
- to use in the following situations:

  o where there is a strong emotional feeling or response;
  o when you are annoyed or irritated by another person or something that has happened; and
  o when you want to tell another person, in a safe way, what you think of them or something about how their behavior is affecting you.

Principles:

A listener will be much more open to really listen if we:

1. Send feelings or perceptions, instead of solutions. For example, rather than saying, "Don't ever take my (book) again" (Message: you are a thief; I don't trust you.)," say, "I get angry when you borrow my book without asking."
2. Take ownership of feelings/perceptions. Blaming or evaluating and judging the other person sets up a wall of anger and defensiveness. Instead of saying, "You are inconsiderate when you borrow my things," say "I get annoyed when you borrow my things without asking."
3. Are open and direct with these feelings or perceptions. Instead of addressing the issue(s) head-on, we often avoid the issue(s) and say one thing while implying another. This avoidance approach will lead either to total isolation or attack and confrontation.

   Use I-Statements as openers not resolvers.

Format:

When you _____
                      (Neutral Description)

I feel _____
                      (No Blame)

And what I would like is _____
                           (Change Request)

   The *when* is followed by a neutral and objective description of the event or another person's behavior. It is important that it does not have any words that imply judgment or evaluation or that may provoke a defensive response, or any possibility of denial by the other person. The statement must be a statement of fact.

   The *I feel* part must use a word or a few words that describe exactly the feeling response of the person making the statement. People often describe how they feel by describing how they want to act (e.g., I feel like withdrawing)

• Important. The feeling must be owned by the person making the statement without blaming or shaming the other person. For example, instead of saying, "I feel you are being defensive," say, "I feel angry when you don't understand my feelings." The *last part* of the statement describes why the person making the statement feels the way he/she does and/or the outcome of change desired.

- Important. There are *no guarantees*. You need to express how you would like for something or a particular behavior to change, but it is not okay to expect or demand that it will happen. It is most effective to spend some time formulating the I statement before using it (Klose & Olivares, 1999).

MINDFULNESS

For a lot of people, the consequence of not keeping up with the flow of their everyday lives through online activities is a heightened sense of anxiety. They fear that if they do not keep up, they will drown in the buildup of work. Mindfulness tackles this by forcing you to stop and think about which pieces of information to engage with and which to ignore. In 2009 we could pay attention on an average of 13 seconds. In 2013 it was 8 seconds—goldfish can focus for 9 seconds. (Hougaard, 2016)

Mindfulness—taking a nonevaluative stance toward thoughts and feelings and allowing thoughts and feelings to come and go, without getting caught up in or carried away by them. (Kabat-Zinn, 2003)

Components

- observing;
- describing;
- acting with awareness; and
- accepting without judgment.

Benefits

- mindfulness increases productivity and decreases stress;
- help decisionmakers make clearer, better quality choices;
- stronger ability to separate relevant from irrelevant information;
- people who are willing to live with unwanted outcomes refrain from doing physical damage to themselves;
- practice a greater sense of self-regulation;
- decreases rumination in thinking;
- decrease stress and increase focus;
- self-compassion;

- increase perspective taking; and
- increases self-reflection (Kabat-Zinn, 2003; Riskin, 2004).

NEUTRAL PHRASES AND QUESTIONS

Neutrality is not making *suggestions* or *judgments*.

As mediators, our job is to help the parties solve their own problems. If we suggest or give our opinions, the parties do not learn to solve problems for themselves. If we judge, the parties will feel as if we are not neutral and they will not trust us.

Instructions

1. Read the following *nonneutral* statements. Decide whether they are S (suggestions) or J (judgments).
2. Rewrite the statements so that they are *neutral*. (The Key Phrases/ Neutral Statements worksheet may be helpful in completing this step.)

- It sounds like you were not playing by the rules.
- Why did you do that? That was a foolish thing to do.
- The best way for you to handle this is to ask your supervisor to move offices.
- It seems that one of you is lying.
- Do you think that you could pay Myosha for the computer?

Examples of Neutral Phrases

Opening and Introductory Statements

- Welcome and thanks for participating in mediation.
- Can you tell us about the situation?
- Can you tell us what happened?
- How are you feeling about that?
- How are you feeling about … (e.g., him having to dominate staff meetings)?

Initial Statements and Two-Way Exchanges

- Can you tell us more about that?
- Would you tell us more about … (how (name) got the computer?)
- What do you mean by …?
- Can you explain more about …?
- Can you give some examples of … (how you think (name) is always messing with you)?
- What happened when …?
- What is different?
- What was it like before?
- Has this problem happened before?
- I feel confused when I hear two different stories. Can we clarify again what happened?
- What would you like to see changed?

Issue Focus and Option Generation

- So, in other words, when (name) says…, you feel …, is that right?
- Is there anything else you'd like to tell us?
- Is there anything else you think might help us today?
- How could you have handled it differently?
- Can you suggest a solution that will resolve the problem of …?
- So, you would agree to …?
- (Name) wants … is there any way you could support that?
- Is that really possible?
- Do you see any way of doing that?
- In the future, how can the problem of … (e.g., keep rumors from spreading)?

General

- You've been very helpful.
- Thank you for being patient.
- Thanks for listening. Now it's your turn.

POSITIONS AND INTERESTS

One of the key elements of mediation is identifying the real interest of the parties. Parties tend to focus and negotiate upon their position or original stance that was established before the mediation process began. Many times, this position is the politically correct position or a problem taken without full knowledge of the other party or their interest. Issues framed out of positions place the parties in an adversarial stance, which does not promote negotiation in the best interest of the parties.

Mediators learn through experience that positions based on preconceived notions change when parties come face to face. Stereotypes are broken down through verbal and nonverbal communication.

An interest indicates needs and wants of the parties, and many times these needs and wants can be reconciled in mediation. Thus, asking the parties what they actually want to accomplish during the mediation will further the process and strengthen the agreement.

During mediation, positions may soften as interests are exposed. Parties may discover a reality they did not know existed via the communication process. Education through face-to-face exposure can bring about a change in the way a person perceives a person or a situation, thereby bringing about a change of position.

Positions	Interests/Needs	Mediator
I don't want to be here	Safety, security	Validate they are in control
I'm mad, enraged	Reassurance, friendship, trust	
Revenge	Fairness	
I'm tough	Security, love	
I don't care	Acceptance, trust	
Confused	Clarification	
Loss of face	Respect, reassurance, reputation	
I'm right	Dominance	
I'm innocent	Empowered	
I'm a victim	Control, empowered	
Just trust me	Reputation, respect	
I'm lonely	Friendship, safety, validation	

REACTING ASSERTIVELY

What does it mean to be aggressive, assertive, or passive?

People are aggressive when they:

- intentionally attack, harm, hurt, put down, or work to take advantage of others;
- believe they are more important than others; or
- believe "get them before they get you."

People are passive when they:

- permit or let others take advantage of them;
- act as if others are more important than them; or
- believe "I should never make anyone feel uncomfortable or displeased except myself."

People are assertive when they:

- express themselves openly and honestly to communicate their needs, wants, feelings, or desires;
- respect the thoughts and feelings of others;
- believe and act that all people are equal; or
- believe "I have a right to ask for what I want."

Many people think there are only two options in responding to a conflict—either be aggressive or be passive. There is a third alternative to engaging in a conflict and that is reacting assertively. Assertiveness is valuable because it allows both parties the opportunity to be respected and to "hear what one another is saying."

PERSONAL PERSPECTIVE ON CONFLICT

1. I intend to use conflict resolution skills in my life in the following ways:

    _____
    _____
    _____
    _____

2.   I pledge to try to be a "peacemaker" and to bring more harmony into: (what and by when)

My own life:

_____
_____
_____
_____

My professional life

_____
_____
_____
_____

Signed: _____

Date: _____

To be reviewed by: _____

SPECIAL PROBLEMS WITH COMEDIATORS

If your partner tells the disputants what they should do to solve the problem:

- take them out and talk with your partner (caucus);
- intervene and ask the disputants to come up with solutions;
- in private, caution your partner not to be a police officer or judge (use with caution);
- lead in the mediation; or
- bring it up in a debriefing mediation meeting.

If your partner takes over and won't let you talk:

- call time out and discuss it with your partner (caucus);
- interrupt quietly and say, "I have say something?";
- talk later with your partner; or
- bring it up at a debriefing mediation meeting.

If your partner takes sides:

- take your partner away and caucus; talk over the situation privately;
- tell your partner not to take sides (use with caution);
- take over the mediation; or
- discuss it at a debriefing mediation meeting.

SPECIAL PROBLEMS WITH DISPUTANTS

What to do if disputants don't talk:

- sit closer to the person who won't talk;
- ask open-ended questions;
- assure the disputants that mediation is confidential;
- ask, "What will happen if you don't resolve this dispute in mediation?";
- state what you think their feelings are; or
- ask, "Would you rather work this out with someone else?"

When you suspect disputants are not telling the truth

- ask the other disputant to comment;
- remind the disputants that they agreed to be honest;
- look for third parties; this no longer is a mediation; get agreement from the disputants to get information from the third party;
- talk to the person alone: caucus;
- tell the person what happens if a disputant is not honest; or
- stop mediation and consult (as a last resort).

When disputants present information that cannot be kept confidential:

- find out more about the situation;
- ask open-ended questions;
- caucus: speak with each disputant individually to find out more information;
- inform the disputants that you will have to tell the proper personnel; or
- discuss the situation with the mediation program coordinator or administrator.

How to deal with MOUs that won't work:

- ask the power down person, "Are you comfortable agreeing to this solution?";
- ask the disputants, "Do you have any additional ideas?";
- ask, "What will happen if you make this agreement?";
- ask if they would agree to another/additional solution;
- talk privately with each disputant in caucus, or
- reality test the MOU.

Disputants who are different from you

- encourage the disputants to recognize their concerns and discuss them;
- recognize the differences and (inside yourself) assess the possible consequences;
- ask the disputants, "How do you think the differences between us are affecting the mediation process?";
- say, "Sometimes people who are very different from one another have difficulty communicating"; or
- ask, "How do you feel about my being a different (race, religion, nationality, sex) from you?" (Klose & Olivares, 1999).

MEDIATION PROGRAMS

Characteristics of a Successful Mediation Program

Mediation programs have been implemented in schools, businesses, and communities. The purpose of these programs is to provide resources that will improve the environment for participants by actively addressing conflicts. Conflicts that are ignored often escalate into aggressive or even violent behavior. Therefore, the management of conflict for conscious, productive outcomes is at the core of a mediation program.

A well-designed program will benefit from the following characteristics:

- a diverse team of conflict managers, who can discern the nature of conflicts and determine the most appropriate dispute resolution strategy to use, will be available;

- skilled mediators are available in a diversity that will accommodate different disputants' biases and needs;
- people in the organization will have knowledge of the availability of the program;
- there will be widespread acceptance of the value of the program;
- administrators, supervisors, and leaders will all support the program;
- appropriate coordinators for the program will be supported.
- conflict managers and coordinators will participate in ongoing training;
- the conflict management program will be considered a part of the organization's improvement plans; and
- external constituencies and supporters will be informed by the program and provide support as necessary.

GLOSSARY

Accommodating: An individual neglects his/her own concerns to satisfy the concerns of the other person.

Active Listening: A communication procedure wherein the listener uses nonverbal behavior, such as eye contact and gestures, as well as verbal behavior, including tone of voice, open-ended questions, restatements, and summaries, to demonstrate to the speaker that he or she is being heard.

Arbitration: Intervention into a dispute by an independent third party who is given authority to collect information, listen to both sides, and make a decision about how the conflict should be settled.

Assertiveness: To state, express, defend, or maintain your wishes, ideas, needs, beliefs, or goals.

Avoidance: The practice of nonengagement.

Basic Needs: Needs that underlie all human behavior, such as survival, self-esteem, belonging, self-actualization, power, freedom, and fun. Like individuals, groups have basic needs, including the need for identity, security, vitality, and community.

Bias: A preconceived opinion or attitude about something or someone. A bias may be favorable or unfavorable.

Body Language: Nonverbal communication expressed by your body.

Conflict Management and Leadership Development Using Mediation
pp. 77–81
Copyright © 2021 by Information Age Publishing
77

Brainstorming: A storm of ideas. A group thinking technique for helping disputants create multiple options for consideration in solving a problem. Brainstorming allows all criticism and evaluation of ideas to be postponed until later.

Clarify: To make clearer or to enhance understanding. With a conflict resolution style/method, open-ended questions are often used for clarification.

Collaboration: Working with the other to seek solutions that completely satisfy both parties. This involves accepting both parties' concerns as valid and digging into an issue in an attempt to find innovative possibilities. It also means being open and exploratory.

Common Interests/Common Ground: Needs and/or interests that are held jointly by the parties in a negotiation.

Community: A social group with common interests, identity, and customs.

Competing: A strategy in which one pursues the satisfaction of his/her own positions or interests at the expense of others—a win-lose approach.

Compromising: Seeking an expedient settlement that only partially satisfies both people. Compromising does not dig into the underlying problem, but rather seeks a more superficial arrangement, e.g., "splitting the difference." It is based on partial concessions.

Conflict: An expressed struggle between at least two interdependent parties who perceive themselves as having incompatible goals, needs, values, ideas, and beliefs. Parties regarding each other as interfering with the achievements of their own goals.

Conflict Responses/Modes: Typical styles of resolution used compromisingly, by individuals. These styles include competing, avoiding, accommodating, and collaborating.

Consensus: An agreement reached by identifying the interests of all concerned parties and then building an integrative solution that maximizes satisfaction of as many of the interests as possible.

Consequences: A result that logically follows an action.

Cooperation: Associating for mutual benefit; working toward a common end or purpose; considers the interests of the other party.

Culture: Those parts of human interactions and experiences that determine how one feels, acts, and thinks. It is through one's culture that one establishes standards for judging right from wrong, for determining beauty and truth, and for judging oneself and others. Culture includes one's nationality, ethnicity, race, gender, sexual orientation, socioeconomic background, age, and physical and mental ability.

Deescalate: To engage in actions that decrease the intensity of a conflict.

Disputant: One who is engaging in a disagreement or conflict.

Diversity: The fact or quality of being distinct.

Empowerment: A method of balancing power in a relationship wherein the lower party acquires more power by gaining expertise, obtaining extra resources, building interpersonal linkages, and/or enhancing communication skills.

Escalate: To engage in actions that increase the intensity of the conflict.

Facilitation: The use of a third party or parties to provide procedural assistance to a group attempting to reach consensus about a problem.

Framing: The manner in which a conflict, solution, or issue is conceptualized or defined.

I Statements: Three-part communication process that describes another person's behavior, your feelings, and requests a behavioral change.

Impartiality: Attitude of the third party; unbiased opinion.

Influence: Power to sway or affect.

Interest/Need: A substantive, procedural, or psychological need of a party in a conflict situation; the aspect of something that makes it significant.

Listening for Feeling: Being able to identify and differentiate facts and feelings.

Managing Emotions: Staying aware of your emotions, biases, and prejudices and realizing their impact on the conflict process.

Mediation: Intervention in a dispute by an impartial third party who can assist the disputants in negotiating an acceptable settlement.

Negotiation: An interaction between two or more parties who have an actual or perceived conflict of interest. In a negotiation, the participants join voluntarily in a dialog to educate each other about their needs and interests, to exchange information, and to create a solution that meets the needs of both parties.

Neutrality: The state of not favoring or biased to either side in a dispute.

Option: An alternative course of action; a possible solution that may satisfy the interests of a party to a dispute.

Peace: A process of responding to diversity and conflict with tolerance, imagination, and flexibility; fully exercising one's responsibilities to ensure that all fully enjoy human rights.

Perception: One's viewpoint or understanding of a situation.

Position: A point of view; a specific solution that a party proposes to meet his/her interests or needs. A position is likely to be concrete and explicit, often involving a demand or threat and leaving little room for discussion. In conflict resolution, an essential activity is for participants to move beyond positions in order to understand underlying interests and needs.

Power: The ability to act or perform effectively; the ability to influence.

Questioning: A skill used to gather meaningful conflict information while not creating a defensive reaction by the disputant.

Reframing: The process of changing how a person or party to a conflict conceptualizes his/her or another's attitudes, behaviors, issues, and interests, or how a situation is defined. Reframing during conflict resolution processes helps to mitigate defensiveness and deescalate tension.

Restating: Skill used to assure accurate understanding of each disputant.

Resolution: A course of action agreed upon to solve a problem.

Summarize: To restate in a brief, concise form. Summarizing is an aspect of active listening used by both disputants and mediators to increase common understanding.

Synergy: Cooperative thought and/or action of two or more people working together to achieve something neither could achieve alone.

Trust: To have confidence in or feel sure of; faith.

Value: A principle, standard, or quality considered worthwhile or desirable.

Violence: Psychological or physical force exerted for the purpose of injuring, damaging, or abusing people or property.

CHAPTER 9

APPENDIX I

Ethical Guidelines for Mediators

These ethical guidelines have been created by the State Bar of Texas Alternative Dispute Resolution Group.

PREAMBLE

These ethical guidelines are intended to promote public confidence in the mediation process and to be a general guide for mediator conduct. They are not intended to be disciplinary rules or a code of conduct. Mediators should be responsible to the parties, the courts and the public, and should conduct themselves accordingly. These ethical guidelines are intended to apply to mediators conducting mediations in connection with all civil, criminal, administrative and appellate matters, whether the mediation is pre-suit or court annexed and whether the mediation is court ordered or voluntary.

GUIDELINES

1.   Mediation Defined. Mediation is a private process in which an impartial person, a mediator, encourages and facilitates communi-

Conflict Management and Leadership Development Using Mediation
pp. 83–88
Copyright © 2021 by Information Age Publishing

cations between parties to a conflict and strives to promote reconciliation, settlement or understanding. A mediator should not render a decision on the issues in dispute. The primary responsibility for the resolution of a dispute rests with the parties.

- Comment: A mediator's obligation is to assist the parties in reaching a voluntary settlement. The mediator should not coerce a party in any way. A mediator may make suggestions, but all settlement decisions are to be made voluntarily by the parties themselves.

2. Mediator Conduct. A mediator should protect the integrity and confidentiality of the mediation process. The duty to protect the integrity and confidentiality of the mediation process commences with the first communication to the mediator, is continuous in nature, and does not terminate upon the conclusion of the mediation.

- Comment (a): A mediator should not use information obtained during the mediation for personal gain or advantage.
- Comment (b): The interests of the parties should always be placed above the personal interests of the mediator.
- Comment (c): A mediator should not accept mediations that cannot be completed in a timely manner or as directed by a court.
- Comment (d): Although a mediator may advertise the mediator's qualifications and availability to mediate, the mediator should not solicit a specific case or matter.
- Comment (e): A mediator should not mediate a dispute when the mediator has knowledge that another mediator has been appointed or selected without first consulting with the other mediator or the parties unless the previous mediation has been concluded.

3. Mediation Costs. As early as practical, and before the mediation session begins, a mediator should explain all fees and other expenses to be charged for the mediation. A mediator should not charge a contingent fee, or a fee based upon the outcome of the mediation. In appropriate cases, a mediator should perform mediation services at a reduced fee or without compensation.

- Comment (a): A mediator should avoid the appearance of impropriety in regard to possible negative perceptions regarding the amount of the mediator's fee in court-ordered mediations.
- Comment (b): If a party and the mediator have a dispute that cannot be resolved before commencement of the mediation as to the mediator's fee, the mediator should decline to serve so that the parties may obtain another mediator.

4. Disclosure of Possible Conflicts. Prior to commencing the mediation, the mediator should make full disclosure of any known relationships with the parties or their counsel that may affect or give the appearance of affecting the mediator's neutrality. A mediator should not serve in the matter if a party makes an objection to the mediator based upon conflict or perceived conflict.

- Comment (a): A mediator should withdraw from mediation if it is inappropriate to serve.
- Comment (b): If after commencement of the mediation the mediator discovers that such a relationship exists, the mediator should make full disclosure as soon as practicable.

5. Mediator Qualifications. A mediator should inform the participants of the mediator's qualifications and experience.

- Comment: A mediator's qualifications and experiences constitute the foundation upon which the mediation process depends; therefore, if there is any objection to the mediator's qualifications to mediate the dispute, the mediator should withdraw from the mediation. Likewise, the mediator should decline to serve if the mediator feels unqualified to do so.

6. The mediation process. A mediator should inform and discuss with the participants the rules and procedures pertaining to the mediation process.

- Comment (a): A mediator should inform the parties about the mediation process no later than the opening session.
- Comment (b): At a minimum the mediator should inform the parties of the following:

(1) the mediation is private (unless otherwise agreed by the participants, only the mediator, the parties and their representatives are allowed to attend);

(2) the mediation is informal (there are no court reporters present, no record is made of the proceedings, no subpoena or other service of process is allowed, and no rulings are made on the issues or the merits of the case); and

(3) the mediation is confidential to the extent provided by law. (See, e.g., $$154.053, and 154.073, Tex. Civ. Prac. & Rem. Code.)

7. Convening the Mediation. Unless the parties agree otherwise, the mediator should not convene a mediation session unless all parties and their representatives ordered by the court have appeared. Corporate parties are represented by officers or agents who have represented to the mediator that they possess adequate authority to negotiate a settlement, and an adequate amount of time has been reserved by all parties to the mediation to allow the mediation process to be productive.

- Comment: A mediator should not convene the mediation if the mediator has reason to believe that a pro se party fails to understand that the mediator is not providing legal representation for the pro se party. In connection with pro se parties, see also Guidelines #9, 11, and 13 and associated comments below.

8. Confidentiality. A mediator should not reveal information made available in the mediation process, which information is privileged and confidential, unless the affected parties agree otherwise or as may be required by law.

- Comment (a): A mediator should not permit recordings or transcripts to be made of mediation proceedings.
- Comment (b): A mediator should maintain confidentiality in the storage and disposal of records and should render anonymous all identifying information when materials are used for research, educational or other informational purposes.
- Comment (c): Unless authorized by the disclosing party, a mediator should not disclose to the other parties information given in confidence by the disclosing party and should maintain confidentiality with respect to communications relating to the subject matter of the dispute. The mediator should report to the court whether or not the mediation occurred, and that

the mediation either resulted in settlement or an impasse, or that the mediation was either recessed or rescheduled.

- Comment (d): In certain instances, applicable law may require disclosure of information revealed in the mediation process. For example, the Texas Family Code may require a mediator to disclose child abuse or neglect to the appropriate authorities. If confidential information is disclosed, the mediator should advise the parties that disclosure is required and will be made.

9.   Impartiality. A mediator should be impartial toward all parties.

- Comment: If a mediator or the parties find that the mediator's impartiality has been compromised, the mediator should offer to withdraw from the mediation process. Impartiality means freedom from favoritism or bias in word, action, and appearance; it implies a commitment to aid all parties in reaching a settlement.

10.   Disclose and Exchange of Information. A mediator should encourage the disclosure of information and should assist the parties in considering the benefit, risks, and the alternatives available to them.

11.   Professional Advice. A mediator should not give legal or other professional advice to the parties.

- Comment (a): In appropriate circumstances, a mediator should encourage the parties to seek legal, financial, tax or other professional advice before, during, or after the mediation process.
- Comment (b): A mediator should explain generally to pro se parties that there may be risks in proceeding without independent counsel or other professional advisors.

12.   No Judicial Action Taken. A person serving as a mediator generally should not subsequently serve as a judge, master, guardian ad litem, or any other judicial or quasi-judicial capacity in matters that are the subject of the mediation.

- Comment: It is generally inappropriate for the mediator to serve in a judicial or quasi-judicial capacity in a matter in which the mediator has had communications with one or more parties without all other parties present. For example, an attorney-mediator who has served as a mediator in a pending litigation should not subsequently serve in the same case as a special master, guardian ad litem, or in any other judicial or quasi-judicial capacity with binding decision-making authority. Notwithstanding the foregoing where an impasse has been declared at the conclusion of a mediation, the mediator, if requested and agreed to by all parties, may serve as the arbitrator in a binding arbitration of the dispute, or as a third-party neutral in any other alternative dispute proceeding, so long as the mediator believes nothing learned during private conferences with any party to the mediation will bias the mediator or will unfairly influence the mediator's decisions while acting in the mediator's subsequent capacity.

13. Termination of Mediation Session. A mediator should postpone, recess, or terminate the mediation process if it is apparent to the mediator that the case is inappropriate for mediation or one or more of the parties are unwilling or unable to participate meaningfully in the mediation process.

14. Agreements in Writing. A mediator should encourage the parties to reduce all settlement agreements to writing.

15. Mediator's Relationship with the Judiciary. A mediator should avoid the appearance of impropriety in the mediator's relationship with a member of the judiciary or the court staff with regard to appointments or referrals to mediation.

CHAPTER 10

APPENDIX II

Captured Conflict Management Phrases

(Organized by phases of the mediation process)

Conflict management phrases from Conflict Management and Dialogue Course at Texas A&M University, Instructor: Dr. Nance T Algert; compiled by Dr. Erin McTigue.

GENERAL PHRASES FOR SEEKING CLARIFICATION

- Help me better understand …
- Explain to me the importance of _____ (a stated position that may represent a bigger issue).
- What are you working to communicate that I am missing?

INITIAL STATEMENTS

- Thank you for making the time to commit to be here today.
- Is it okay if I call you by your first name? (Note: Create balance in names—first names for all or titles for all.)
- We (mediators) are not here to make judgments as to who may be right or wrong. Nor are we here to propose solutions to the prob-

Conflict Management and Leadership Development Using Mediation
pp. 89–94
Copyright © 2021 by Information Age Publishing

lems. Our goal is to support you as you work through differences, find areas of common ground, propose solutions and ultimately prepare a written agreement.

- One goal of mediation is for us to create an opportunity for you to share what is happening in your workplace, from your perspective.

RULES AND ROLES

- As mediators, one of our critical roles is creating and maintaining a productive and safe space for you to solve problems. To achieve that goal, we all must agree to a standard set of rules, which we take the time to review to insure common understanding for all.
- "Operating Principles" (can be a substitute for rules)
- While this is a confidential process, there are a few limits to confidentiality.
- Categories of issues that are beyond the scope of mediation are: _____
- If you share information that leads us to believe that you may harm yourself or others, we must stop the mediation, break confidentiality, and seek help.
- This is what you can expect from us: _____
- This is what we expect from you: _____
- Are you clear what you can expect from _____ (M1) and me?
- What are you looking to get from this process?
- (Particularly in situations where people may feel forced to attend mediation) I understand that you may have felt some pressure to attend, but once here, you have the power and control to use this time to engage in moving forward in the process.
- It is important to note that the generation of a MOU greatly increases the likelihood of success for participants to follow through with solutions.

INITIAL STATEMENT OF CONFLICT
(AND GENERAL RESTATEMENT PHRASES)

- Before you begin to engage in problem solving, we are going to have each of you share from your perspective what you brought you into mediation.

- This is the opportunity for you to share what is happening in your workplace from your perspective ...
- What brings you to mediation?
- Help us to understand what your relationship look liked in the past and how it has changed?
- When was the shift in the working relationship?
- Please be patient with me as I write this down.
- Let me check for understanding.
- Through your lens ... (Use as a preface to restate a person's narratives).
- Did I miss any critical pieces? (Note: check "exhaustively")
- Is it fair for me to capture this as ...
- Thank you for the clarification ...
- (To the second person who presents). Often times the second person who shares spends a good deal of energy refuting the narrative of the first person. Try to resist that tendency. It is more productive if you present your narrative independently, and within your own framework of understanding.

PRESENTING JOINT NARRATIVE

- Please actively listen for new information from your colleague.
- Additionally, look for potential areas of common ground.

ISSUE DEFINITION

- Now to move us to the next phase of the process, we are going to spend time for each of you to define the *specific* issues you wish to work on today.
- Person X, an issue that you would like to discuss today is ...?
- How would you like to word that?
- Is that part of issue #1 or is that a separate issue?
- Have I captured that correctly?
- Would you allow me to collapse that _____ into one issue?

THOUGHTS AND FEELINGS

- You both now have some new information.
- Let's begin with elements of common ground.
- Between the two of you, there are four issues (note inclusive language).
- What are your thoughts and feelings to what Person X said?
- There seems to be a strong emotion associated with X, can you describe that?
- Are you in a place that you can speak directly to him/her?
- Can you restate what X said?
- What do you need X to understand?
- Please elaborate more on _____ issue.
- You are actually moving to the next step of the process.
- Would you like me to write that down as a potential option?

OPTION GENERATION

- You have had a rich discussion on _____ and many thoughts and feelings have been explored. I wonder if you are both at a point to generate options.
- What does tomorrow look like in working together?
- What do you need from X?
- Is this something that I should write down for a potential MOU?

MEMORANDUM OF UNDERSTANDING

- The MOU generation is entirely up to you. It is not a legal document but is a good faith effort.
- Items should be specific and realistic. You should share a common understanding of the items.
- The goal of writing this down formally is so that both parties clearly understand the commitments made today.
- Parties that generate a MOU have a higher likelihood of following through compared to unwritten goals that they make.
- During option generation, you have said X, Y, and Z. How would you like me to capture this in a MOU?

- You will each get a copy of the MOU and no other copies will be made. What is your plan for sharing the MOU, if at all, beyond this meeting? For example, some participants feel it would be useful to share a copy of their MOU with their administrator.
- How would you like it to be shared at the end of this meeting? Do you want to take the MOU together, send it as a memo, et cetera?

CLOSURE

- I have tremendous respect for your time and effort today to help build a better work environment. You are clearly very committed to your work and workplace.
- Often it is easier to stay embattled than to come and talk about your thoughts and feelings.
- To help in insuring confidentiality, it can be useful to rehearse for potential future situations. What could you say if tomorrow a mutual colleague, who is aware of the mediation meeting, asks you, *"How did the mediation go? I'm so curious!"*
- What's your message when you go back to the group?

SPECIAL TOPIC: HANDLING INTERRUPTIONS

- I know that you are anxious to respond. There will be ample time for you to share your thoughts and feelings.
- _____ deserved the opportunity to speak uninterrupted.
- I want to remind you of your note pad to jot down important thoughts so that you don't forget them.

SPECIAL TOPIC: HANDLING RAMBLING

- Let me interrupt (not, I'm sorry, to interrupt).
- I know that I'm interrupting, but I would like us to refocus on …
- I know that I've interrupted, but I'm going to take this opportunity to summarize …

OTHER HELPFUL PHRASES

- "Aspirant goals": What are your "aspirant goals" for the day? These are my aspirant goals for the day _____.
- "Mediation belongs to the disputants; the process belongs to you."
- Someone may "cost you more energy" than other someone.

REFLECTIVE PROMPTS

- How do I minimize the impact of my bias on others' process?
- How do we use language for moving parties forward?
- In reflection, separate "I didn't do my best" versus "I made a mistake." Ask: Can I do anything about it? If no. Then, what can I learn?

PHRASES WHEN YOU ARE A DISPUTANT IN A CONFLICT

- Person X, when you said _____, this wasn't likely your intention, but I felt _____. Can we talk about this?
- Clearly, I cost you a lot of energy when I did _____.
- Can we return to a dialogue on _____?

SOME OTHER THOUGHTS TO REMEMBER

- Anger at the right time is justified, but it can't become you.
- At times we need to have integrity to say "no."
- The last of human freedoms—the ability to choose one's attitude in a given set of circumstances.

CHAPTER 11

APPENDIX III

Reading Reference List

CHANGE

Algert, N. E., & Watson, K. (2005, April). *Systemic change in engineering education: The role of effective change agents for women in engineering.* Proceedings: Women in Engineering Advocates Network/National Association of Minority Engineering Professionals Advocates Conference, Las Vegas, NV.

Betty. (2007, August, 11). A primer on privilege. [Web log post] Study and serviceable. http://brown-betty.livejournal.com/305643.html

Burke, W. W. (2002). *Organization change: Theory and practice.* SAGE.

Clark, B (2004). *Sustaining change in universities.* SRHE and Open University Press.

Change. (n.d.). *Cambridge Academic Content Dictionary.* http://dictionary.cambridge.org/dictionary/american-english/change_1

Chism, N. V. N. (1998). The role of educational developers in institutional change: From the basement office to the front office. *To Improve the Academy, 17,* 141–153.

Gioia D. A., & Thomas, J. B. (1996). Strategic change in universities. *Administrative Science Quarterly, 41*(3), 370–403. http://www.jstor.org/stable/2393936?seq=1

Johnson, S. (2002). *Who moved my cheese?* Penguin Putnam.

Kotter, J. P. (2008). *A sense of urgency.* Harvard Business Review.

Lencioni, P. (2006). *The five dysfunctions of a team.* John Wiley & Sons.

Maurer, R. (n.d.). *Resistance to change—Why it matters and what to do about it.* http://www.rickmaurer.com/wrm/

Conflict Management and Leadership Development Using Mediation
pp. 95–105
Copyright © 2021 by Information Age Publishing
All rights of reproduction in any form reserved.

CONFLICT CULTURES

Blake, R., & Mouton, J. S. (1964). *The managerial grid*. Gulf.

Chen, X., Zhao, K., Liu, X. (2012): Improving employees' job satisfaction and innovation performance using conflict management. *International Journal of Conflict Managemen,t 23*(2), 157–172.

Gelfand, M., Leslie, L., Keller, K., & Dreu, C. (2012): Conflict cultures in organizations: How leaders shape conflict cultures and their organizational-level consequences. *Journal of Applied Psychology, 97*(6), 1131–1147.

Goldin, I., & Mariathasan, M. (2014). *The butterfly defect: How globalization creates systemic risks, and what to do about it*. Princeton University Press.

Montes, C., Rodriguez, D., & Serrano, G. (2012). Affective choice of conflict management styles. *International Journal of Conflict Management, 23*(1), 6–18.

Roche, W., & Teague, P. (2012). Do conflict management systems matter? *Human Resource Management, 51*(2), 231–258.

Saeed, T., Almas, S., Anis-ul-Haq, M., & Niazi, G. S. K. (2014). Leadership styles: Relationship with conflict management styles. *International Journal of Conflict Management, 25*(3), 214–225.

Shonk, K. (2018, May 7). How to deal with cultural differences in negotiation. *Program in Negotiation Harvard Law School*. [Blog post]. https://www.pon .harvard.edu/daily/business-negotiations/how-to-deal-with-cultural-differences-in-negotiation/?utm_source=WhatCountsEmail&utm_medium=daily&utm_date=2018-05-07-13-55-00&mqsc=E3955001

Watson, N. T., Xie, L., & Etchells, M. J. (2018). *Cultural impact on conflict management in higher education*. Information Age.

Zhang, X. A., Cao, Q., & Tjosvold, D. (2011). Linking transformational leadership and team performance: A conflict management approach. *Journal of Management Studies, 48*(7), 1586–1611.

CONFLICT MANAGEMENT, RESOLUTION, AND STRATEGIC ENGAGEMENT

Adrian-Taylor, S. R. (2007). Conflict between international graduate students and faculty supervisors: toward effective conflict prevention and management strategies. *Journal of Studies in International Education 11*(1), 90–117.

Algert, N. E. (2007). Conflict management. *Effective Practice for Academic Leaders, 2*(9), 1–16.

Algert, N. E., & Froyd, J. (2002). Effective decision making in teams. *The Foundation Coalition*. https://drive.google.com/file/d/1H9TJQb1EHVYmkgZM3C-4pz3bKTbEDoyB/view

Algert, N. E., & Froyd, J. (2002). Effective intrapersonal and interpersonal communication. *The Foundation Coalition*. https://drive.google.com/file/d/1OrPxfL4QTmVsm-bHElbP9N5gvfqmxTL-/view

Algert, N. E., & Froyd, J. (2002). Understanding conflict and conflict management. *The Foundation Coalition*. https://drive.google.com/file/d/11eWkcHks_RKAUVSn5sNiMc9W9TpPXOs6/view

Algert, N. E., & Stanley, C. A. (2007, September). Conflict management. *Effective Practices for Academic Leaders*, *2*(9), 1–16.

Algert, N. E., & Watson, K. (2002). *Basic mediation training*. The Center for Change and Conflict Resolution.

Algert, N. E., & Watson, K. (2002). *Conflict management: Introductions for individuals and Organizations*. The Center for Change and Conflict Resolution.

Alper, S., Tjosvold, D., & Law, K. S. (2000). Conflict management, efficacy, and performance in organizational teams. *Personnel Psychology*, *53*(3), 625–642.

Aschenbrenner, C. A., & Siders, C. (1999). Managing low-mid intensity conflict in the health care setting. http://www.freepatentsonline.com/article/Physician-Executive/102286870.html

Amason, A. C., Thompson, K. R., Hochwater, W. A., & Harrison, A. W. (1995). Conflict: An important dimension in successful management teams. *Organizational Dynamics*, *24*(2), 20–35.

Baldridge, J. V. (1971). *Power and conflict in the university*. Wiley.

Bailey, D. (1998). Life in the intersection: Race/ethnic relations and conflict resolution. *The Fourth R*, *78*, 18–19.

Baron, R. A. (2001). Positive effects of conflict: A cognitive perspective. *Employee Responsibilities and Rights Journal*, *4*(1), 25–36.

Beck, M. (2001). *Finding your north star: Claiming the life you were meant to live*. Three Rivers Press.

Bissell, B. (2003, February). *Handling conflict with difficult faculty tools for maintaining your sanity and your dignity*. Retrieved from www.AAHEBulletin.com

Borg, M., et al. (2011). Conflict management in student groups: A teacher's perspective in higher education. *Hogre utbildning*, *1*(2), 111–124. http://lup.lub.lu.se/luur/download?func=downloadFile&recordOId=2270096&fileOId=2862084

Carmichael, G., & Malague, M. (1996, February). *How to resolve conflicts effectively*. Paper presented at the Fifth Annual International Conference for Community & Technical College Chairs, Deans, and Other Organizational Leaders. Phoenix, Arizona. (ERIC Document Reproduction Service Number ED 394 572)

Chew, P. K. (Ed.). (2001). *The conflict and culture reader*. NYU Press.

Cipriano, R. (2011). *Facilitating a collegial department in higher education: Strategies for success*. Josey-Bass.

Coffman, J. R. (2009). Conflict management for chairs. *Department Chair*, *20*(1), 18–21.

Cloke, K., & Goldsmith, J. (2000). *Resolving conflicts at work: A complete guide for everyone on the job*. Jossey-Bass.

Cloke, K., & Goldsmith, J. (2000). *Resolving hidden and organizational conflict: Stories of transformation and forgiveness*. Jossey-Bass.

Conflict Dynamics Profile. (n.d.) Retrieved from the Center for Conflict dynamics at Eckerd College website: http://www.conflictdynamics.org/products/conflictdynamics.php

Cowan, D., Palomares, S., & Schilling, D. (1994). *Conflict resolution skills for teens*. Innerchoice.

Crawford, D., & Bodine, R. (1996). *Conflict resolution education: A guide to implementing programs in schools, youth-serving organizations and community and juvenile justice settings—Program report* (p. D-1). Office of Juvenile Justice and Delinquency Prevention,U.S. Department of Justice/Safe and Drug-Free Schools Program, U.S. Department of Education.

Crookston, R. K. (2014). Using conflict to achieve true peace. *The Department Chair, 25(2)*, 22–25. https://doi.org/ 10.1002/dch.20069

Doelker, R. E., Jr. (1989). Mediation in academia: Practicing what we preach. *Mediation Quarterly, 7(2)*, 157–161.

Di Virgilio, F., & Di Pietro, L. (2012). *The role of organizational culture on informal conflict management.* http://ssrn.com/abstract=1978428

Duryea, M. L. (1992). *Conflict and culture: A literature review and bibliography.* University of Victoria Institute of Dispute Resolution.

Fisher, R., & Ury, W. (1986). *Getting to yes: Negotiating agreement without giving in.* Houghton Mifflin Harcourt.

Folger, J. P., & Poole, M. S. (1984). *Working through conflict: A communication perspective.* Scott, Foresman, and Company.

Fox, S., Spector, P. E., & Miles, D. (2001). Counterproductive work behavior (CWB) in response to job stressors and organizational justice: Some mediator and moderator tests for autonomy and emotions. *Journal of Vocational Behavior, 59*(3), 291–309. http://citeseerx.ist.psu.edu/viewdoc/download?doi= 10.1.1.424.1987&rep=rep1&type=pdf

Gelfand, M. J., Leslie, L. M., Keller, K., & de Dreu, C. (2012, November). Conflict cultures in organizations: How leaders shape conflict cultures and their organizational-level consequences. *Journal of Applied Psychology, 97(6)*, 1131–1147.

Girard, K., & Koch, S. J. (1996). *Conflict resolution in the schools: A manual for educators.* Jossey-Bass.

Glasl, F. (1982). *Conflict management: a guide for leadership and consultants.* Verlag Paul Haupte.

Global Hive/Ruche Mondiale. (2014). Youth engagement in context. *Youth engagement.* http://globalhive.ca/hubs/youth_engagement.pdf

Gerzon, M. (2007). *Leading through conflict: How successful leaders transform differences into opportunities.* Harvard Business School.

Green Carmichael, S. (2010). Difficult conversations: 9 common mistakes. *Harvard Business Review.* https://hbr.org/2010/10/difficult-conversations-9-common-mistakes

Gmelch, W.H. (1991, October). *The creation of constructive conflict within educational administration departments.* Paper presented at the annual meeting of the University Council for Educational Administration, Baltimore, Maryland.

Gmelch, W. H., & Carroll, J. B. (1991). The three Rs of conflict management for department chairs and faculty. *Innovative Higher Education, 16*, 107–123.

Harrison, T. R. (2007, March). My professor is so unfair: Student attitudes and experiences of conflict with faculty. *Conflict Resolution Quarterly, 24(3)*, 349–368.

Hickson, M., & McCroskey, J. C. (1991, October). Diagnosing communication problems of academic chairs: Applied communication in context. *ACA Bulletin, 78*, 8–13.

Higher Education Program and Policy Council. (n.d.). http://facultysenate.tamu
.edu/Quick_Links/Shared_Governance_in_Colleges_and_Universities.pdf

Holton, S. (1995). Conflict 101. *New Directions in Higher Education*, *1995*(92), 5–10.

Jehn, K. A., Rupert, J., & Nauta, A. (2006). The effects of conflict asymmetry on mediation outcomes. *International Journal of Conflict Management*, *17*(2). http://dx.doi.org/10.1108/10444060610736594

Jenkins, R. (2010, July 22). The four quadrants of administrative effectiveness. *The Chronicles of Higher Education*. http://chronicle.com/article/The-Four-Quadrants-of/123642/?sid=at&utm_source=at&utm_medium=en

Johnson, D. W., & Johnson, R. T. (1987). *Creative conflict*. Interaction Books.

Johnson, D. W., & Johnson, R.T. (1995). *Teaching students to be peacemakers*. Interaction Books.

Jordan, T. (2000). *Glasl's nine-stage model of conflict escalation*. Mediate.com. http://www.mediate.com/articles/jordan.cfm

Kabanoff, B. (1987). Predictive validity of the MODE conflict instrument. *Journal of Applied Psychology*, *72*, 160–163.

Karpman, S. (1967). The drama triangle. *Fairy tales and script drama analysis, Transactional Analysis Bulletin*, *7*, 26.

Kegan, R. (1981). *The evolving self: Problem and process in human development*. Harvard University Press.

Kegan, R., & Lahey, L. L. (2009). *Immunity to change: How to overcome it and unlock the potential in yourself and your organization*. Harvard Business Press.

Kelley, H. H. (1987). Toward a taxonomy of interpersonal conflict processes. In S. Oskamp & S. Spacapan (Eds.), *Interpersonal processes* (pp. 122–147). SAGE.

Klingel, S., & Maffie, M. (2011, August/October). Conflict management systems in higher education: A look at mediation in public universities. *Dispute Resolution Journal*, 12–17.

Kilmann, K. W. (1988). The conflict-handling modes: Toward more precise theory. *Management Communication Quarterly*, *1*(3), 430–435.

Kochman, T. (1981). *Black and White styles in conflict*. University of Chicago Press.

Lan, Z. (1997). A conflict resolution approach to public administration. *Public Administration Review*, *57*(1), 27–35.

Lankoff, G. (2004). *Don't think of an elephant: Know your values and frame the debate*. Chelsea Green.

Likert, R., & Likert, J. G. (1976). *New ways of managing conflict*. McGraw Hill.

Linabary, J. R., Krishna, A., & Connaughton, S. L. (2017). The conflict family: Storytelling as an activity and a method for locally led, community-based peacebuilding. *Conflict Resolution Quarterly*, *34*(4), 431–453.

Lord, R. G., Klimoski, R. J., & Kanfer, R. (Eds.). (2003). *Emotion in the workplace: Understanding the structure and role of emotions in organizational behavior*. Jossey-Bass.

Malhotra, D., & Bazerman, M. (2007). *How to overcome obstacles and achieve brilliant results at the bargaining table and beyond*. Bantam Books.

Marques Santos, C., Uitdewilligen, S., & Passos, A. M. (2015). Why is your team more creative than mine? The influence of shared mental models on intra-group conflict, team creativity, and effectiveness. *Creativity & Innovation Management*, *24*(4), 645–658.

McElveen, N. M., Leslie, P., & Malotky, D. (2006). Ethical issues in faculty conflict. *Teaching Ethics*, 7(1), 33–56. https://www.uvu.edu/ethics/seac/

McNamara, R. (2013). *The elegant self: A Radical approach to personal evolution for greater influence in life*. Performance Integral.

Meyers, S. A., Bender, J., Hill, E. K., & Thomas, S. Y. (2006). How do faculty experience and respond to classroom conflict? *International Journal of Teaching and Learning in Higher Education*, 18(3), 180–187. http://www.isetl.org/ijtlhe/

Mindell, A. (2000). *The leader as martial artist: Techniques and strategies for revealing conflict and creating community*. Lao Tse Press.

Miller, T. (2015). *Conflict management for department chairs*. Paper presented for a conflict management course on conflict management and dialogue, Texas A&M University, College Station, TX.

Morrison, J. (2008). The relationship between emotional intelligence competencies and preferred conflict-handling styles. *Journal of Nursing Management*, 16(8), 974–983.

Northrup, T. A. (1995). *The uneasy partnership between conflict theory and feminist theory*. Unpublished manuscript. Syracuse, NY: Syracuse University.

Olsen, D., & Near, J.P. (1994). Role conflict and faculty life satisfaction. *Review of Higher Education*, 17(2), 179–195.

Opotow, S. (1989). *The risk of violence: Peer conflicts in the lives of adolescents*. Paper presented at the annual convention of the American Psychological Association, New Orleans, LA.

Otey, R. G. (1999). The effect of peer mediation on discipline problems as perceived by administrators, teachers, and counselors at selected high schools in region XX, education service center (Order No. 9943549). http://search.proquest.com/docview/304571957?accountid=7082

Pammer, W. J., & Killian, J. (Eds.). (2003). *Handbook of conflict management* (p. 58). Marcel Dekker.

Patterson, K., Grenny, J., McMillan, R., & Switzler, A. (2011). *Crucial conversations: Tools for talking when stakes are high* (2nd ed.). McGraw-Hill.

Putnam, L. L. (1995). Formal negotiations: The productive side of organizational conflict. In A. M. Nicoreta (Ed.), *Conflict and organizations: Communicative processes* (pp. 183–200). State University of New York Press.

Putnam, L. L. (1994). Beyond third party role: Disputes and managerial intervention. *Employee Responsibilities and Rights Journal*, 7, 1–23. https://doi.org/10.1007/BF02621058.

Restate. (n.d.). *Merriam-Webster Dictionary*. http://www.merriam-webster.com/dictionary/restate

Reybold, L. E. (2005, December). Surrendering the dream. Early career conflict and faculty dissatisfaction thresholds. *Journal of Career Development*, 32(2), 107–121.

Riemer, S., Muller, C., Virányi, Z., Huber, L., & Range, F. (2013). Choice of conflict resolution strategy is linked to sociability in dog puppies. *Applied Animal Behaviour Science*, 149(1–4), 36–44.

Robbins, S.P. (1974). *Managing organizational conflict*. Prentice-Hall.

Robbins, S. P., Finney, M. I., & O'Rourke, J. (2008). *The truth about winning at work*. Pearson Education. https://books.google.com/books?id=4

5hbz7xrYsYC&printsec=frontcover&source=gbs_ge_summary_r&cad =0#v=onepage&q&f=false.

Rosenberg, M. (2003). *Nonviolent communications: A language of life*. Puddle Dancer Press.

Rouhana, N. R., & Korper, S. H. (1996, October). Case analysis: Dealing with the dilemmas posed by power asymmetry in intergroup conflict. *Negotiation Journal*, *12*(4), 353–336.

Ruble, T. L., & Thomas, K. W. (1976). Support for a two-dimensional model of conflict behavior. *Organizational Behavior and Human Performance*, *16*, 143–155.

Scharmer, O. C. (2009). *Theory U: Leading from the future as it emerges*. Berrett-Koehler.

Scholtes, P. R., Joiner, B. L., & Streibel, B. J. (2003). *The team handbook*. Oriel.

Schrage, J., & Giacomini, N. G. (2009). *Reframing campus conflict*. Stylus.

Spangle, M., & Robyn, E. (2014, Winter). Managing conflict in academic settings. *ACResolution Magazine*. http://www.acresolution-digital.org/acresolutionmag/ winter_2014/?pm=2&u1=friend&pg=48#pg48

Stanley, C., Watson, K., & Algert, N. E. (2005). A faculty development model for mediating diversity conflicts in the university setting. *Journal of Faculty Development*, *5*(3), 129–142.

Stanley, C. A., & Algert, N. E. (2007). An exploratory study of the conflict management styles of department heads in a research university setting. *Innovative Higher Education*, *32*(1), 49–66.

Stevens, R. E., Williamson, S., & Tiger, A. (2013). Conflict resolution strategies in an academic setting. *Feature Edition*, *2013*(4), 10–21.

Stone, D., Patton, B., & Heen, S. (2010). *Difficult conversations: How to discuss what matters most* (Rev. ed.).   Penguin Books.

The Office—Conflict Resolution (Episode Highlight). (2017, August 9). *Mediation and Use of I-statements*. https://youtu.be/Xg3dAmhFJdE

Thomas, K. W. (1992). Conflict and conflict management. *Journal of Organizational Behavior*, *13*(3), 265–274.

Thomas, K. W., & Kilmann, R. H. (1974). *Thomas-Kilmann conflict mode instrument*. Xicom.

Tidd, S. T., McIntyre, H. H., & Friedman, R. A. (2004). The importance of role ambiguity and trust in conflict perception: Unpacking the task conflict to relationship conflict linkage. *The International Journal of Conflict Management*, *15*, 364–380.

Ting-Toomey, S. (2005). The matrix of face: An updated face-negotiation theory. In W. B. Gudykunst (Ed.), *Theorizing about intercultural communication* (pp. 71–92). SAGE.

Tolle, E. (1997). *The power of now: A guide to spiritual enlightenment*. Namaste.

Trombly, R. M., Comer, R. W., & Villamil, J. E. (2002, April). Case III: Managing conflict—The case of the faculty stuck in the middle. *Journal of Dental Education*, *66*, 533–540.

Ursiny, T. (2003). *The coward's guide to conflict: Empowering solutions for those who would rather run than fight*. Sourcebooks.

Yarn, D. (2014). Designing a conflict management system for higher education: A case study for design in integrative organizations. *Conflict Resolution Quarterly, 32*(1), 83–105.

Watson, N., & Watson, K. (2011). *Conflict management: An introduction for individuals and organizations.* The Center for Change and Conflict Resolution.

Watson, N. T., & Watson, K. (2011). *Basic mediation training book* (2nd ed.). The Center for Change and Conflict Resolution.

Watson, N. T., Watson, K. L., & Stanley, C. A. (2017). *Conflict management and dialogue in higher education: A global perspective* (2nd ed.). Information Age.

Wilber, K. (2001). *A theory of everything: An integral vision for business, science, and spirituality.* Shambhala Publications.

Wilber, K. (2007). *The integral vision: A very short introduction to the revolutionary integral approach to life, god, the universe, and everything.* Shambhala.

William U., Brett, J., & Goldberg S. (1998). *Getting disputes resolved.* Jossey-Bass.

Womack, D. F. (1988). A review of conflict instruments in organizational settings. *Management Communication Quarterly, 1*(3), 437–445.

Womack, D. F. (1988). Assessing the Thomas-Kilmann conflict MODE survey. *Management Communication Quarterly, 1*(3), 321–349.

Wright, K. L., Etchells, M. J., & Watson, N. T. (2018). Meeting in the middle: Eight strategies for conflict mediation in your classroom. *Kappa Delta Pi Record, 54*(1), 30–35. https://doi.org/10.1080/00228958.2018.1407174

Xicom Incorporated. (1996). *Conflict workshop facilitator's guide.*

LEADERSHIP AND MANAGEMENT

Acuna, A. (2013). *How much time do managers spend on conflict?* Learning4Managers. https://learning4managers.com/dir/conflict_management/.

Ames, D. R., & Flynn, F. J. (2007). What breaks a leader: The Curvilinear relation between assertiveness and leadership. *Journal of Personality and Social Psychology, 92*(2), 307–324.

Bennett, J. B., & Figuli, D. J. (1993). *Enhancing departmental leadership: The roles of the chairperson.* The Oryx Press.

Blake, R., & Mouton, J. (1964). The managerial grid: The key to leadership excellence. Gulf.

Bolman, L. G., & Gallos, J. V. (2011). *Reframing academic leadership.* Jossey-Bass.

Booth, D. B. (1982). *The department chair: Professional development and role conflict.* American Association for Higher Education.

Bowman, R. F. (2002, January/February). The real work of department chair. *The Clearing House, 75,* 158–162.

Bowman, R. F. (1999). Community as the organizing principle. *Catalyst for Change, 28,* 23–24.

Comer, R. W., Haden, N. K., Taylor, R. L., & Thomas, D. D. (2002). Leadership strategies for department chairs and program directors: A case study approach. *Journal of Dental Education, 66*(4), 514–519.

Finkin, M. W., & Post, R. C. (2009, March). *For the common good: Principles of American academic freedom.* Yale University Press.

Gmelch, W. W. (1991). Paying the price for academic leadership: Department chair tradeoffs. *Educational Record, 72*(3), 45–48.

Hougaard, R., Carter, J., & Coutts, G. (2016). *One second ahead: Enhance your performance at work with mindfulness.* Springer.

Metcalf, H., & Urwick, L. (Eds). (n.d.). *Dynamic administration.* Harper.

Lumpkin, A. (2004). Enhancing the effectiveness of department chairs. *Journal of Physical Education, Recreation & Dance, 75*(9), 44–48.

Marquardt, M. J. (2014). *Leading with questions.* George Washington University.

McLaughlin, G. W., Montgomery, J. R., & Malpass, L. F. (1975). Selected characteristics, roles, goals, and satisfactions of department chairmen in state and land-grant institutions. *Research in Higher Education, 3*, 243–259.

Nafukho, F., Wawire, N., & Lam, P. (2011). *Management of adult education organizations in Africa.* UNESCO and Pearson Education.

Project Management Institute. (n.d.). http://www.apics-chicago.org/downloads/ Supply_Chain_Management_&_Change_Management.pdf

Reddick, L, Jacobson, W., Linse, A., & Young, D. (2005). A framework for inclusive teaching in STEM disciplines. In M. L. Ouellett (Ed.), *Teaching inclusively: Resources for course, department & institutional change in higher education* (pp. 435–450). New Forums Press.

Tichy, N. M., & Devanna, M. A. (1986). *The transformational leader.* Wiley.

Wilson, V. (1999). *The department chair: Between a rock and a hard place.* (ERIC Document Reproduction Service No. ED 430 458).

MEDIATION ISSUES

Aggarwal, P., Rochford, L., & Vaidyanathan, R. (2009). The hot seat: Profiling the marketing department chair. *Journal of Marketing Education, 31*(1), 40–51. https://doi.org/10.1177/0273475308324089

Barrett, J. T., & Barrett, J. (2004). *A history of alternative dispute resolution: The story of a political, social, and cultural movement.* Wiley.

Beck-Kritek, P. (1994). *Negotiating at an uneven table.* Jossey-Bass.

Charkoudian, L., Ritis, C. D., Buck, R., & Wilson, C. L. (2009). Mediation by any other name would smell as sweet—Or would it? The struggle to define mediation and its various approaches. *Conflict Resolution Quarterly, 26*(3), 293–316.

Cloke, K. (2001). *Mediating dangerously: The frontiers of conflict resolution.* Jossey-Bass.

Cloke, K., & Goldsmith. (2000). *Resolving personal and organizational conflict: Stories of transformation and forgiveness.* Jossey-Bass.

Cobb, S. (1993). Empowerment and mediation: A narrative perspective. *Negotiation Journal, 9*(3), 245–259.

Cohen, J. (1997). *Making dispute resolution sessions accessible to people with disabilities. SPIDR News, 21*(2), 1, 14–15.

Fisher, R., & Ury, W. (1981). *Getting to yes: Negotiating agreement without giving in.* Houghton Mifflin.

Gibson, J. W. (1994). *Mediation: Basic training program.* Sam Houston State University.

Gibson, J. W. (1995). *Advanced conflict resolution training*. Sam Houston State University.

Girard, K., & Koch, S. J. (1996). *Conflict resolution in the schools: A manual for educators*. Jossey-Bass.

Gravois, J. (2006). Mob rule: In departmental disputes, professors can act just like animals. *Chronicle of Higher Education, 5*(2), 92.

Kabat-Zinn, J. (2003). Mindfulness-based interventions in context: Past, present, and future. *Clinical Psychology: Science and Practice, 10*(2), 144–156.

Klose, R., & Olivares, R. (1999). *Bryan ISD peer mediation training guide*. Bryan Independent School District.

Maddus, R. B. (1995). *Successful negotiation*. Crisp.

McCormick, M. A. (1996). Confronting racism as a mediator. *Society of Professionals in Dispute Resolution, 20*(3), 1, 8.

Moore, C. (n.d.). How mediation works. *The mediation process: Practical strategies for resolving conflict*.

New Mexico Center for Dispute Resolution. (1990). *Basic mediation and peer mediation training guide*.

Office of Special Counsel, U.S. Gov. (2015). Alternative dispute resolution. https://osc.gov/Pages/ADR.aspx.

Riskin, L. L. (2004). Mindfulness: Foundational training for dispute resolution. *Journal of Legal Education, 54*, 79.

Satir, V., & Banmen, J. (1991). *The Satir model: Family therapy and beyond*. Science & Behavior Books.

Stanley, C. A., Watson, K. L. & Algert, N. E. (2005). A faculty development model for mediating diversity conflicts in the university setting. *Journal of Faculty Development, 20*(3), 129–142.

Warters, W. C. (1999, December). *Mediation in the campus community: Designing and managing effective programs*. Jossey-Bass Press.

Young, P. M. (2006). Rejoice-rejoice-rejoice, give thanks, and sing: ABA, ACR, and AAA adopt revised model standards of conduct for mediators. *Appalachian Journal of Law, 5*, 195, 209–219.

ABOUT THE AUTHOR

Nance founded The Center for Change and Conflict Resolution (CCCR) in 1995, and as president of CCCR, she provides consulting, counseling and conflict management services. She consults and facilitates groups with an emphasis of capacity building for individuals and organizations. Nance's areas of expertise include effective communication, conflict management and diversity, change management and organization development.

Nance is a former assistant dean for organization development and diversity initiatives in the College of Education and Human Development and a former director for climate enhancement initiatives for the vice president for diversity. She currently works part time as a professor of practice in the College of Veterinary Medicine and Biomedical Sciences and as a clinical professor in the Department of Education Administration and Human Resource Development at Texas A&M University. Nance has a PhD in educational psychology, is a licensed professional counselor, is in the Association for Conflict Resolution Academy of Advanced Practitioners, and a fellow in the American Psychotherapy Association.

Dr. Algert's overarching professional commitment is to support individuals and organizations in honing their power to accomplish their personal and professional goals.

Printed in the United States
By Bookmasters